William Shakespeare

AS YOU LIKE IT

Penny Gay

NORTHCOTE

BRITISH
COUNCIL

© Copyright 1999 by Penny Gay

First published in 1999 by Northcote House Publishers Ltd, Horndon House, Horndon, Devon PL19 9NQ, United Kingdom.
Tel: +44 (01822) 810066 Fax: +44 (01822) 810034.

Reprinted 2007

British Library Cataloguing-in-Publication Data
A catalogue record for this book is available from the British Library

ISBN 978-0-7463-0910-0

Typeset by PDQ Typesetting, Newcastle-under-Lyme
Printed and bound in the United Kingdom

WRITERS AND THEIR WORK

ISOBEL ARMSTRONG
General Editor

AS YOU LIKE IT

For Virginia Gay,
another Rosalind

Contents

Biographical Outline

1564	William Shakespeare born in Stratford-upon-Avon, Warwickshire; third child of John Shakespeare, glover and wool-dealer, and Mary Arden.
1582	Marries Anne Hathaway in Stratford; children Susanna, born 1583, twins Hamnet and Judith, born 1585. (Hamnet dies in 1596.)
c. 1587	Becomes an actor in London (family remains in Stratford).
c. 1590	Shakespeare's first plays performed. Publication of Lodge's *Rosalynd*.
1593–4	Publication of Shakespeare's narrative poems *Venus and Adonis*, *The Rape of Lucrece*.
1599	Opening of the Globe Theatre; probable first performance of *As You Like It*.
c. 1614	Shakespeare ceases playwriting; retires to Stratford.
1616	Dies (April 23) and is buried in Stratford's Holy Trinity church.
1623	Publication of First Folio of Shakespeare's complete works, including first publication of *As You Like It*

Note on Texts Used

All quotations from *As You Like It* are keyed to the Arden edition of the play, edited by Agnes Latham (London: Methuen, 1975; repr. London and New York: Nelson, 1996). Other quotations from Shakespeare's plays are taken from *The Norton Shakespeare*, edited by Stephen Greenblatt, Walter Cohen, Jean E. Howard and Katharine Eisaman Maus (New York and London: W. W. Norton & Company, 1997).

Quotations from Thomas Lodge's *Rosalynd* are taken from the edition of Brian Nellist (Keele University: Ryburn Publishing, 1995).

1

Prologue

A play which announces itself 'As You Like It' to all appearances
sets out to please its audience. It also gives away no clues as to its
subject matter: no exciting history, no pathos-inducing representation of the fall of a great man. All 'plays', of course, promise
pleasure of a sort, otherwise we would not pay out good money
to see them; but comedies depend for their attractiveness less on
their subject matter and more on the simple guarantee of a good
time in the theatre.

William Shakespeare, as a playwright and shareholder in the
Lord Chamberlain's Men, the company of the Globe Theatre,
was committed to fulfilling that guarantee: that much, at least,
we can infer about the man who spent his working life in
London and then retired to his birthplace of Stratford-upon-
Avon as a prosperous 'gentleman'. Although there is no record
of *As You Like It*'s performance during Shakespeare's lifetime
(or, indeed, for over a century after), it was printed among his
comedies in the First Folio of 1623, and scholars have confidently
assigned the probable year (1599) and casting of the major male
roles in its first production. Rosalind, one of the longest roles in
the Shakespearean canon, would have been played by an
adolescent boy, as would all the other female parts.

Was *As You Like It* performed to an Elizabethan or Jacobean
audience? *Did* it please? Since the play is demonstrably aware of
its own theatricality, my analysis of it works with the hypothesis
of its being written for a 1599 Globe audience, but it must be
stressed that this is no more than an exercise in historical
imagination. This book depends on an 'if...' (though, as
Touchstone says, 'much virtue in If' (5. 4. 102)). My views as
to how the play might have affected its first audience are based
on close reading of the text informed by the current (late

1

twentieth-century) state of historical scholarship and theory concerning the play. We indulge in this study partly because the play is 'by Shakespeare', a figure of immense cultural importance: if we can demonstrate our relation to him we demonstrate our own intellectual and spiritual weight. But above all, *As You Like It* remains playable and readable, 400 years after it was written – that is, it enables us to make stories that are meaningful to ourselves and our communities.

COMEDY, CRITICISM, AND HISTORY

Criticism, like performance, is a kind of story-telling, a making of meaning. Critical work on Shakespeare's comedies began in the eighteenth century within the context of contemporary literary and aesthetic theory: Dr Johnson, for example, wrote of *As You Like It*, 'the fable is wild and pleasing.... The comick dialogue is very sprightly... and the graver part is elegant and harmonious.'[1] Appreciation of the playwright's character-drawing and a sense of his profound humanity and moral wisdom were the keynotes of nineteenth-century criticism, and, indeed, of much in the twentieth century, with the addition of a developing interest in formal structures and the intricacies of poetic imagery. By and large, the critical project for the last 200 years has been a totalizing enterprise, an effort to define the 'meaning' of the play in terms of the 'essential' human values that its text presented.

More recent criticism, however, alerts us to the political agenda directing this aesthetic aim: as Gary Waller points out, 'All societies attempt to regulate the arts, directly and indirectly....There are, therefore, historically or culturally *dominant* meanings, readings that we (or our teachers or powerful critics) prefer.'[2] Such readings tend to reinforce a conservative view of society, and of theatre's place in it: romantic comedy, ending in wedding and feasting, is recuperative, it offers an achievable image of the community at its best. It celebrates the values of love, generosity, forgiveness, tolerance of human failings. This is a seductive view, and at one level I have no quarrel with it: comedy is where we go when we want to be reassured that things can sometimes turn out for the

2

best (a 'feel-good' movie performs the same function). But beyond this pleasant valley there lies the mountain of moral seriousness which supposedly gives educational gravitas to our experience of Shakespearean comedy. Gary Waller again offers a helpful formulation: there is

> a kind of criticism that claims to be 'historical', but finds the plays' meanings in 'universals', truths or insights that are supposedly always true, and in a sense located outside history. Much traditional thematic criticism that discusses plays in terms of such ahistorical abstractions as appearance and reality, the maturing of true love, or the discovery of an underlying personal identity – as if these were unaffected by historical factors of race, class, or gender – is criticism of this type. Any claim to such universality is difficult to maintain since it endows the observer with an ability to step outside of history.[3]

As observers – whether readers, actors, or audience of the text – we cannot dehistoricize our own position. Thirty years ago I might have written an elegant essay on *As You Like It* and the human desire for wholeness through marriage and incorporation into a regenerated community. My argument would still have been drawn from close readings of the playtext, perhaps tricked out with some quotations from Renaissance neo-Platonism if I wished to make a claim that the play had the same 'meaning' to its first audience (though I probably wouldn't have been very interested in the role of the play as something for consumption by a theatre audience). This reading would have been no more and no less 'true' than the reading which is proposed in the following pages.

What this book offers is an assessment of what now seem useful meanings at the end of the twentieth century, in the light of changes in thinking about the past and about literature and theatre, changes which stress issues of gender, class, and the slippery relation of words to 'meaning'. It raises the question of what we are doing when we engage in the representation of human actions, for example, in the theatre – though it proposes no answer beyond a recognition of our current fascination with such representation, something which we apparently share with the original Elizabethan theatre-goers. 'All the world's a stage', says Jaques, 'And all the men and women merely players' (2. 7. 139–40). The stage, the men and women on it, may be imagined

3

differently, but the metaphor of life as a series of performances remains seductively meaningful.

The direction of much late-twentieth-century criticism was set by C. L. Barber in 1959: his book *Shakespeare's Festive Comedy* was the first sustained attempt to relate the comedies to the society in which they were produced, through the application of anthropological ideas. Today the most prevalent scholarly approach to Shakespeare, descended from such work as Barber's (and in England from the work of the marxist critic Raymond Williams) is the 'new historicist', that is, a reading of Shakespeare's plays in a matrix of other Elizabethan and Jacobean texts, the object being to illuminate the social, political and other discourses to which they all contribute. Steven Mullaney, for example, in *The Place of the Stage* (1988), formulates his project thus:

> literary analysis is conceived not as an end in itself but as a vehicle, a means of gaining access to tensions and contradictions less clearly articulated in other cultural forums but all the more powerful for their partial occlusion. Literature itself is conceived neither as a separate and separable aesthetic realm nor as a mere product of culture, but as one realm among many for the negotiation and production of social meaning, of historical subjects, and of the systems of power that at once enable and constrain those subjects....the culture of any given historical period is conceived as a heterogeneous and irreducibly plural social formation, and as a dynamic process of representation and interpretation rather than a fixed ensemble of meanings and beliefs.[4]

I have made use of Mullaney's investigations into these processes particularly in chapter 3, though typically as a postmodern reader I have played verbal games with them in order to pursue my own notion of the play's meanings. Mullaney's work on the 'rhetoric of space in Elizabethan London' has provided me with a productive pun on 'liberty', a word which resonates in the last lines of Act 1: 'Now go we in content/To liberty, and not to banishment', as the young women and the clown exit to Arden. It would seem fairly obvious, indeed 'natural', to see Arden as the place of freedom for all, a green world as C. L. Barber and Northrop Frye called it, redolent of fertility and rebirth; at the very least, an escape into pastoral fantasy where it is always summer. But contrast the

4

thinking of Fiona Shaw and Juliet Stevenson, who played Celia and Rosalind in Adrian Noble's 1985 production of the play:

> the traditional conception of Arden [is] a kind of theatrical Arcadia reminiscent of Suffolk, full of logs and boughs and rivers of trout, where the inhabitants slap their thighs, jump off stumps and wear feathered caps at a jaunty angle. The play is so clearly not a rural romp, and Shakespeare's description of the forest bears no relation to the familiar or recognisable – it is a 'desert' and 'uncouth', it is referred to as bleak and barren, but also as containing lionesses and snakes like a jungle or plain; it seems to be a strange, weird realm which has the power to transform itself, and in which all things are possible. It is both an image from our nightmares and a place of infinite potential. Above all, we felt, it is a metaphor. But a metaphor for what exactly? ... If it is a realm of the imagination, then of whose imagination?[5]

The notion of 'liberty' is obviously very much complicated by these ideas; so too is our sense of the autonomy of those who escape into Arden. (In chapter 6, I discuss the differences that arose between Shaw and Stevenson – as feminist actresses – and Adrian Noble as paternalist director, within even this unconventional interpretation of 'Arden'.)

Other modern readings, for example that of Christine Edzard's film (1992), align Arden with the marginal world of society's drop-outs – their 'liberty' being only to starve or to freeze. Historicist scholarship which I discuss in chapter 3 suggests that this may have been a resonance of the play's pastoral scenes available to its first audiences, aware of the disastrous effects of changing agricultural practices in the English Midlands. But such political overtones cannot, one feels, have entirely displaced the pleasure provided by the romantic fable and its comic confusion – though even romance is problematized by new historicists: Waller, for example, claims, 'Over and over again, the comedies show the precariousness of the institutions by which desire is socialized'.[6] Little attention is paid by most historicist critics to the specific experience offered by theatre: the audience member's experience as an individual *and* as a member of a group, in that particular space and period of time. *As You Like It* offers not only a narrative of socialization, but also (in the courtship scenes) a visual and aural, moment-by-moment embodiment of the workings of desire. And the

5

specificities of this experience are the decisions of the actors, at that time, in that place. But as Anthony B. Dawson observes, 'the very contingency of performance in whatever venue generates uncontrolled interpretations. The materiality of the theater thus contributes to its heterogeneity, indeed is essential to it.'[7] There is no final control over how a member of the audience is affected by what he or she hears and sees in the theatre. Some may laugh, and some may weep, at the very same scene, depending on their own relation to the issues they see embodied.

Stephen Greenblatt, the most influential figure in American new historicism, in his essay 'The Circulation of Social Energy' has attempted to formulate a relation between the experience of theatre and issues that concern the society at large:

> If there is no expressive essence that can be located in an aesthetic object complete unto itself, uncontaminated by interpretation, beyond translation or substitution – if there is no mimesis without exchange – then we need to analyze the collective dynamic circulation of pleasures, anxieties, and interests. This circulation depends upon a separation of artistic practices from other social practices, a separation produced by a sustained ideological labor, a consensual classification.[8]

It follows from Greenblatt's theorizing about the 'separate' work that is done through and by theatre that the labour of the producers of that work must be acknowledged. In the pages that follow I have tried to give recognition – indeed, honour – to the actors who have made meaning with *As You Like It* over the past 400 years; I have done this either by quoting or referring to their interpretations of particular moments in the play, or by imagining what a modern actor might do with a line or scene. My imagination no doubt is feeble in this respect, since I have not made acting my profession, but the exercise is illuminating, even though what I am doing is no more than what William Worthen calls realizing the 'formalities latent in modern performance practice, formalities of behavior that re-textualize the play within the conventions of contemporary theatre'.[9] Those conventions will include embodiments of sexual desire, of class and gender conflict, of comic and pathetic behaviours; no amount of historical imagination can truly relocate us with the sixteenth century's perspective on these things.

How then can we think about the pleasure which *As You Like*

It both offers and, historically, has provided? Once again, it is to the actors' work that we must turn. The plot, the 'old tale', may provide some suspense, but we enjoy more seeing (safely) a representation of violence and heroic masculinity in, for example, Orlando's unlikely wrestling triumph. The playscript may demonstrably provide wit (which will bring a mental smile to the reader), but the clown or the witty, wordy woman on stage will make us laugh with its utterance. The romance between Orlando and Rosalind may be enjoyable to read, but to watch actors' embodiment of this extraordinary courtship is to experience something unique. In 1994 I wrote,

> Like Orlando, we would – if we had time in the bustle of the plot and the excess of linguistic riches – stop and ask ourselves, which do we fancy more, Rosalind or Ganymede? Does it matter? The pleasure of the actor's multi-gendered presence (for this safe, enclosed moment of performance time) is delicious.[10]

Reading or play-going, despite (or perhaps because of) my explorations in history and theory, I haven't lost that pleasure. I hope that this book will assist readers to find their own pleasure in the playtext.

2

There Comes an Old Man Had Three Sons

As the audience hears the opening lines of *As You Like It* – 'As I remember, Adam, it was upon this fashion...' – they will mentally settle back with the comfortable sense that this will, indeed, be a play as they like it: they have heard this story, or one very similar, innumerable times before. It is the folktale of the Youngest Brother, the young man who, deprived of anything but his native wit, strength, and innocence, after many adventures wins riches, renown, and the hand of the fairest lady in the land.[1] Some part of the original Elizabethan audience of the play – the part that could read, and afford to buy books – would have been familiar with Thomas Lodge's popular romance novel *Rosalynd*, first published in 1590 and republished in 1592, 1596, and 1598; this is the immediate origin of the plot of Shakespeare's play. But most audiences – whether Elizabethan, Victorian, or modern; whether English, European, or Asian – will respond as Celia does in 1. 2. 110 to Le Beau's enthusiastic gossip about the 'old man and his three sons': 'I could match this beginning with an old tale'.

That the play takes a 180-degree swerve from being 'Orlando's story' to being, so emphatically, Rosalind's *play*, is simply the first of the many subversive delights that it offers. If Orlando speaks the opening words, claiming our attention to his situation, we might expect him to end the story. The Royal Shakespeare Company's production in 1989 played with just this expectation: Orlando stepped forward to speak the Epilogue, had a fit of stage-fright, and Rosalind came to his rescue – speaking lines presumably very different from the formal conclusion Orlando would have uttered. And even before the astonishing postscript of the Epilogue, Orlando is silenced earlier than Rosalind is in the main body of the play. His last line is 'If there be truth in sight, you are my Rosalind' (5. 4. 118) – an acknowledgement of the power of the 'magic' she has brought about. After this he quietly takes his place in the social hierarchy which enjoins silence before the more powerful male figure, Duke Senior.

Rosalind's unexpected power is not in evidence, however, until Act 2 and her taking up the role and costume of a boy. Shakespeare spends Act I developing the image of the oppressive and violent society from which Orlando and Adam, and Rosalind and Celia, will flee. It is a masculine society in which men compete for power, usurping the rights and property of their brothers. Orlando's opening complaint to Adam stresses that his brother has broken his promise to their dead father, failing to educate him or to provide him with the means to live as a gentleman. Orlando is consequently in danger of losing his 'gentility', his class status, as he is forced to 'feed with [Oliver's] hinds' or farm-labourers (1. 1. 18–19). Such eloquent and bitter verbal complaints make no impression on Oliver – language, we see, is powerless unless reinforced by social status: Orlando's resort to physical violence is the natural result. Deeds are more powerful than words in the world in which the play opens.

Oliver, securely ensconced in his position of social dominance, is able to call on a surrogate to do his deeds for him: Charles the wrestler. Charles himself is an honourable man, simply using his natural strength to get a living: he is not tainted by the corrupt nature of this society but acts as a conduit for its power-structures. If the socially superior figure of Oliver tells him of Orlando that 'there is not one so young and so villainous this day living', Charles immediately determines to 'give him his payment' (1. 1. 152–8) without further question of the nature of Orlando's supposed villainy. But Charles also is a conduit for more benign forces: he tells Oliver (and the audience) that Frederick has banished the old Duke, 'whose lands and revenues enrich the new Duke' (1. 1. 102–3). The irony of the echo of Oliver's behaviour towards Orlando is apparently lost on the guileless Charles, though perhaps not on Oliver, who seems to change the subject rather abruptly at this point – 'What, you wrestle tomorrow before the new Duke?' (1. 1. 120).

9

Louis A. Montrose, in an influential essay first published in 1981, argued that Orlando's situation had particular resonances for the original audience of the play, an audience whose ideology was firmly patriarchal – who would, that is to say, have a social and political interest in observing Orlando's situation and in the sleight of hand which the playwright uses to resolve it. Rather than seeing Act 1 as a series of plot devices to get everyone into the Forest of Arden, Montrose argues that 'what happens to Orlando in the forest is Shakespeare's contrivance to remedy what has happened to him at home'.[2] As a younger son he was in a very problematic social situation: 'The expected social fate of a gentleborn Elizabethan younger son was to lose the ease founded upon landed wealth that was the very hallmark of gentility'[3] because of the custom of primogeniture which dictated that the eldest son should inherit the estate, thus keeping it unfragmented. 'The process of comedy', Montrose points out – and specifically the plot-devices of Lodge's *Rosalynd*, whereby the portionless younger son wins the hand of the Duke's daughter (thus gaining status *and* revenue), and the villainous older son is converted to a virtuous life[4] –

> works against the seemingly inevitable prospect of social degradation suggested at the play's beginning. . . . Shakespeare uses the machinery of pastoral romance to remedy the lack of fit between deserving and having, between Nature and Fortune.[5]

Montrose writes illuminatingly of the father–son bond basic to a patriarchy, as well as of the rivalry between brothers. 'The comedy. . . reaffirms a positive, nurturing image of *fatherhood*.'[6] He points out that Orlando is quick to establish himself as a young man worthy to join the all-male court-in-exile in the forest; he 'attend[s] the Duke at dinner' (4. 1. 170) in preference to spending time playing courting games with Ganymede – he literally knows on which side his bread is buttered. 'Before Orlando is formally married to Rosalind at the end of the play, he has reaffirmed the fraternal and filial bonds in communion with other men.' Even 'Orlando's rescue of Oliver from the she-snake and the lioness frees the brothers' capacity to give and receive love'[7] – indeed, they become 'blood brothers'.[8] And it is finally *through marriage*, Montrose points out, that the bonds between siblings and between generations (fathers and children

– there are no mothers in this text) are transformed and renewed, in an elegantly chiasmatic patterning: 'the younger brother weds the daughter of the elder brother, and the elder brother weds the daughter of the younger brother'.[9] The play has been the story of Orlando's passage from youth to adulthood: 'By the end of the play, Orlando has been brought from an impoverished and powerless adolescence to the threshold of manhood and marriage, wealth, and title'.[10]

Montrose's historicist approach, in which the playtext is read alongside a number of other non-fictional texts from the period to illuminate dominant discourses, helps us to see the source of the ongoing power of the folktale of the dispossessed young man. Every society in which money and inheritance are controlled by a system of male bonds will recognize the dynamic at work in the *structure* of the play. Montrose concludes, however, by speculating,

> In the world of its Elizabethan audience, the form of Orlando's experience may indeed have functioned as a collective compensation, a projection for the wish-fulfilment fantasies of younger brothers, youths, and all who felt themselves deprived by their fathers or their fortunes. But Orlando's mastery of adversity could also provide support and encouragement to the ambitious individuals who identified with his plight...For the large number of youths in Shakespeare's audience – firstborn and younger siblings, gentle and base – the performance may have been analogous to a rite of passage, helping to ease their dangerous and prolonged journey from subordination to identity, their difficult transition from child's part to adult's.[11]

There is a leap here from sober historicism (the quotation of a 1600 document complaining that 'plays and theatres' are the cause of 'disorder & lewd demeanours which appear of late in young people of all degrees') to a wish-fulfilment of the writer's own: the unquestioned assumption that the play's important audience consisted of the young males. More recent research has shown that there were significant numbers of women in the audience, and middle-aged people of both sexes.[12] No doubt even such a varied audience would register, consciously or unconsciously, the conservative and reconciliatory structure of the basic narrative played out before them that Montrose has identified. But they would also have observed, and felt, a great deal more

11

which is not so easily contained – not least, the female *agency* through which this reconciliation of men is brought about.

'LIKE JUNO'S SWANS...COUPLED AND INSEPARABLE'

Montrose's reading of the play takes the commodification of women as absolute: structurally, in this model, they are silent and unprotesting as they are handed from father to son. On stage, it is a very different matter. Women – or the boy actors representing them – talk, for the two hours' traffic that makes up the audience's theatrical experience. 'Do you not know I am a woman? when I think, I must speak', cries Rosalind in one of the play's many moments of deconstructive pleasure (3. 2. 245). This disruptive habit of speaking what is on their minds is already evident in the play's first-act exposition of masculine power and social bonds.

Once again it is Charles the wrestler who provides us with useful information about the play's themes: 'never two ladies loved as they do' (1. 1. 112). The close bond between Celia and Rosalind is in some sense a direct result of the usurpation by Celia's father of Rosalind's father's dukedom: Rosalind has a home but no parents (the usurping Duke's 'love' for her, as reported by Charles, is evidently only for show); she has only one person on whom to lavish her familial affection, her cousin Celia. Some modern productions of the play have suggested, more or less explicitly, that there is a lesbian relationship between the two cousins – Le Beau's remark to Orlando that their 'loves/Are dearer than the natural bond of sisters' (1. 2. 265–6) can be appropriately inflected by the actor – and in a modern-dress production this would be a perfectly acceptable interpretation of the relationship (though the plot's implication that each woman is then 'saved' for heterosexuality could be seen as both crass and offensive). But if we are attempting to understand the range of possible meanings proposed by the text when it was first written and performed, then the question of the precise way the cousins' noticeably great affection is visually expressed is irrelevant. Taking a cue from Montrose, we might even propose that their more-than-sisterly love suggests a small utopian space within the oppressive masculine court; it is unaffected by social hierarchies (older/younger, patron/dependent) – such a society as the exiled Duke and his co-mates claim to have achieved in the forest. Celia certainly seems to think of their relationship in these terms: 'You know my father hath no child but I, nor none is like to have; and truly when he dies, thou shalt be his heir; for what he hath taken away from thy father perforce, I will render thee again in affection' (1. 2. 16–19). What we see, in 1. 2 and 1. 3, is two young women who – in the private space which the stage becomes as soon as they step onto it – talk without restraint, and without the power-driven agenda which underlies the speeches of Orlando, Oliver, and Duke Frederick. Instead they talk of merriment, and agree to 'devise sports' (1. 2. 23). Two are proposed: Rosalind's 'what think you of falling in love?' and Celia's more cautiously philosophical 'Let us sit and mock the good hussif Fortune from her wheel' (1. 2. 30–31). The second option is the one that is immediately taken up (since 'falling in love' requires an object, and one is yet to appear), and, with the aid of the court jester Touchstone and the officious courtier Le Beau, a dazzling display of verbal wit cascades from the two young women. It could clearly go on indefinitely, but that there is already a plot whose impetus cannot be stayed: Le Beau's 'news' is of *masculine* 'good sport' (1. 2. 92), brutal fighting only slightly ritualized – as Touchstone drily remarks, 'It is the first time that ever I heard breaking of ribs was sport for ladies' (1. 2. 127–9). Nevertheless they stay to witness it, thus allowing their female space to be invaded by men and become public space – and the encounter with masculinity to begin which will provide the conditions for 'falling in love'.

During the wrestling and immediately thereafter both Celia's and Rosalind's private wit is restrained into notably decorous femininity – 'We pray you for your own sake to embrace your own safety and give over this attempt' (1. 2. 167–8) – and/or breathless exclamations – 'O excellent young man!' (1. 2. 201). Equally notably, as the play for the first time moves from prose into blank verse, a sense of formality constrains the public utterances of the young women as they attempt to convey their warm interest in Orlando. The women's formal gestures – Celia's congratulations and Rosalind's giving of a chain – silence Orlando as well:

Can I not say, 'I thank you'? My better parts
Are all thrown down, and that which here stands up
Is but a quintain, a mere lifeless block.

(1. 2. 239–41)

The masculine world of violent rivalry – whose language also invades Rosalind's speech ('Sir, you have wrestled well, and overthrown/More than your enemies', 1. 2. 244–5) – cannot provide the space for the elaborate game of 'falling in love' with all its witty feints and catches. A neutral space, gendered neither masculine nor feminine, must be found if male and female are to meet and progress beyond the formal constraints of patriarchal supervision.

Just like Orlando, the girls are almost obsessively aware of their fathers in the play's first act. Present, absent, or dead, it doesn't matter, they are still the guarantors of identity for these young people; all utterances that are not just 'sport' are given authority by reference to them (e.g. Celia's declaration of love for Rosalind, quoted above, 1. 2. 7–21). So much is this theme harped on that an attentive audience may spot the first sign of a change, a development towards full adulthood, in Rosalind's reply to Celia's 'But is this all for your father?' – 'No, some of it is for my child's father' (1. 3. 10–11): she is beginning to imagine herself as a parent (and wife) rather than a child. Later, in the liberty of the forest, this rejection of the father's power to give meaning to her life becomes the full-blown declaration 'But what talk we of fathers, when there is such a man as Orlando?' (3. 4. 34–5).

In the apparent non-sequitur of the second part of Rosalind's utterance in 1. 3. 11 we may also observe another hint as to the direction the play is going to take. 'O how full of briers is this working-day world!' she sighs. Despite the 'sports' provided both by the public masculine world of the court and by the private witty space of the young women and their jester, there is no true 'holiday', or time for recreation, laughter, self-discovery, love, possible in the world of the play as we have so far encountered it. The young women's private space is always subject to invasion by the 'working-day world' – the world in which the pursuit of power, status, and affluence is the dominant drive of the males who rule it. And that is exactly what we see at 1. 3. 36:

14

Enter Duke [Frederick] with lords.
CELIA With his eyes full of anger.
DUKE F. *[to Rosalind]* Mistress, dispatch you with your safest haste
And get you from the court.

His reason for banishing Rosalind harps still on fathers, since Rosalind is only significant as a rival's heir: 'Thou art thy father's daughter, there's enough' (1. 3. 54). Celia's response is the significant one here: 'Shall we be sunder'd? Shall we part, sweet girl?/No, let my father seek another heir' (1. 3. 94–5). In a radical denial of public values, she rejects her father's authority in favour of mutual affection between herself and her friend. But that will have to be fully experienced in another place, 'the Forest of Arden', where they will 'seek [Celia's] uncle' (1. 3. 103), Rosalind's father. (Though, as we soon see, the charms of the holiday world of Arden and their own female establishment give this latter intention to re-establish themselves in relation to a father-figure very low priority.)

The act ends with a sense of excitement in both girls' speeches: anything seems possible, once they have decided to leave the patriarchal domain. Their decisions as to disguise symbolize the two fields of contestation identified by Montrose: Celia will take a massive drop in class status, from princess to 'poor and mean' woman; Rosalind will change gender, leaving the role of daughter/niece to take upon herself that of the male adolescent. These apparently radical changes can be achieved simply through an alteration in costume: appearance and behaviour determine identity (as we know from historians' work on Elizabethan sumptuary laws), there is no 'natural' or essential determinant of class or gender. A 'swashing and a martial outside' will be enough to signal masculinity, 'poor and mean attire' low class (1. 3. 116, 107).

It follows that such changes in identity require new names: instead of the names given them by their (god-)parents as they were inducted into the Christian church, the girls re-baptize themselves according to their *chosen roles*:

CELIA What shall I call thee when *thou art a man*?
ROSALIND I'll have no worse a name than Jove's own page,
And therefore look you call me Ganymede.
But what will you be call'd?
CELIA Something that hath a reference to *my state*.

No longer Celia, but Aliena.

(1. 3. 119–24, my emphases)

This will not be the last time that we will see the two young women implicitly flout the authority of the patriarchal church (see chapter 6). Another act of renaming triumphantly ends the scene: what Duke Frederick decrees as 'banishment' is for Celia and Rosalind 'liberty'. The audience can only agree that anything would be better than this oppressive and violent environment.

3

The Skirts of the Forest

As You Like It was probably one of the first plays staged at the Globe, which opened as a state-of-the-art theatre in 1599 with the motto *Totus mundus agit histrionem* – a version of which may be heard in Jaques' famous set-piece in Act 2, 'All the world's a stage'. The new theatre was built, as were most other places of entertainment, in the 'liberties' or suburbs, the area outside the jurisdiction of the walled city of London, but close enough to be a mere bridge or ferry-ride away, across the river on the Thames's south bank. Steven Mullaney, in his historical study *The Place of the Stage: License, Play, and Power in Renaissance England*, argues that

> long before the emergence of popular drama, the Liberties of London had served as a transitional zone between the city and the country, various powers and their limits. . . as a culturally maintained domain of ideological ambivalence and contradiction. . . .When popular drama moved out into the Liberties, it appropriated this civic structure and converted the moral license and ambivalence of the Liberties to its own ends, translating its own cultural situation into a liberty that was at once moral, ideological, and topological – a freedom to experiment with a wide range of ideological perspectives and to realize, in dramatic form, the cultural contradictions of its age. . . .
>
> It was to the Liberties, according to Stow [a contemporary observer], that citizens retired to pursue pastimes and pleasures that had no proper place in the community. . . . What was lodged outside the city was excluded, yet retained; denied a place within the community, yet not merely exiled. . . .the margins of the city served as a more ambivalent staging ground: as a place where the contradictions of the community, its incontinent hopes and fears, were prominently and dramatically set on stage.[1]

Building on this observation, we can speculate that when the play's original audience heard Celia say, at the end of Act 1, 'Now go we in content,/To liberty, and not to banishment', they might have felt a frisson of the special exploratory and potentially transgressive experience which 'going to the theatre' literally offered them. I am going to propose a reading of *As You Like It* which extends Mullaney's arguments about the marginality of the theatre into a kind of phenomenology of the gaze. The 'gaze', according to modern theorists,

> is bound up with formations and operations of subjectivity. This means that the gaze is not simply the mechanism of perception, but rather a fundamental structure in the ways in which the subject relates to the cultural order, and, perhaps even more significantly, the way in which subjectivity itself is formed through the mechanisms of the gaze.[2]

Not only is the audience in Shakespeare's theatre *in* a marginal and excitingly libertarian place, they are also *looking at* a representation of destabilized centres and margins, and thus being looked at or *positioned* by what is being done and said by the bodies of actors on the stage. They are taking part in a carnivalesque negotiation of the symbiotic relation between the official discourse of the city or court and the world of the underclass, outlaws.

The idea of women or other relatively powerless members of the audience taking their 'liberty' at and through the theatre bears investigating, especially in relation to the extraordinary phenomenon of Shakespeare's women-centred comedies. Mullaney unfortunately does not choose to analyse the implications of his historicism with regard to women either as members of the audience or as represented on the stage. His study deals with male-oriented texts which are more obviously 'about' power (*Henry IV, Measure for Measure*). But, as Stephen Orgel points out, in Elizabethan social hierarchy everyone except the Queen was 'feminized' – i.e. dependant – in relation to someone else;[3] adolescent youths, for example, were virtually of the same status as women (as Rosalind/Ganymede says, 'boys and women are for the most part cattle of this colour', 3. 2. 402–3). This expands productively the specific argument of Montrose that we looked at in chapter 2, regarding the story of the dispossessed younger brother, and allows us to 'read' the play more in terms

18

of what we actually see on stage, not what we may unconsciously or otherwise infer about the play's negotiation of relations between men.

Performances at the south bank theatres were always in the afternoon, to take advantage of the even shadow cast on the north-east facing stage; it was the audience who were in sunlight, particularly those directly opposite the front of the stage – what would be considered the 'best' position these days in an indoor proscenium-arch theatre (you may see such people at the new Globe in London today, vainly shielding their eyes against the sun, while those who have chosen a position at the 'side' of the stage revel in their easy sightlines and sense of closeness to the actors, who of course play as much to the 'side' as to the front). The stage, largely covered by a roof called 'the heavens', held up by two onstage pillars which served for the trees which Orlando 'mars' with his love-songs, was a vast space, some 1,160 sq. ft (106 sq. m). Actors entered and exited via two doors in the tiring-house wall at the back of the stage. There *may* have been a third, central, door at the Globe – or a space for 'discoveries' to be shown – but the two-door hypothesis is the simpler and more elegant model, and is what is shown in the only contemporary illustration of an Elizabethan theatre, the 'De Witt' drawing of the Swan. I want to suggest that each of these doors, during the course of each play, took on a specific significance which assisted the audience in reading the symbolic meanings of the play, while at the same time the actors were enabled by the 'stage directions' encoded in the dialogue to know which door to use for each entrance and exit.[4]

Briefly, one door represented 'further inward', that is, towards the inner sanctum, the seat of power of the society represented in the play's story. The other, naturally, represented 'further outward' from the locale assumed for each scene: from the court to the town, for example. This 'outwards' door tends to be used by the lower-status characters in a play – those who have errands or work to do – as contrasted with the inwards door's association with the most powerful and aristocratic figures in the play, who rarely have to do anything beyond entering and giving commands, then returning to their sanctum. We can see that this pattern would operate easily in Act 1 of As You Like It, with Oliver and Duke Frederick usually coming onto the stage from the 'inwards' door, and Orlando using the 'outwards' door for his entrances and exits. In 1. 2 both Touchstone and Le Beau would come from the 'inwards' door since they are the bearers of messages from Duke Frederick, who in due course arrives with his retinue from the same place, invading, as we saw in chapter 2, the space which had for the duration of the earlier part of the scene been established as the women's private area. As long as Rosalind and Celia are under the protection of Duke Frederick, they also use the 'inwards', privileged door, but their exit in the last scene of the act is clearly signalled as a change: 'Now go we in content / To liberty, and not to banishment'. From this point onwards in the play, they will be associated with the 'outwards' door, leaving the 'inwards' door still associated with the tyrannous Duke.

What then does the audience see and understand as Act 2 begins? *'Enter Duke Senior, Amiens, and two or three lords like foresters.'* The Duke is the person of highest status in the forest, and this will be immediately made clear by his entering with his retinue from the 'inwards' door. Further, there will be a striking moment of recognition if (as is often the case in modern productions) Duke Senior and his evil brother are played by the same actor. Duke Frederick's two other brief appearances are (a) in 2. 2, after Duke Senior's exit 'outwards' to look for Jaques – his brother re-enters through the door of authority; and (b) 3. 1, a scene demanding a quick change and re-entrance through the 'inwards' door. Even without the doubling, this pattern of entrance and exit provides a frisson of anxiety in the audience as it begins to 'see' the way power is performed: whether benignly or viciously, it is still power.

Act 2 scene 3 is a good example of the internal stage directions: if Orlando and Adam enter from separate doors, meeting, it is clear that Adam comes on from the 'inwards' door – he is still part of Oliver's household, as opposed to the already exiled Orlando. Adam's speeches emphasize this: 'Come not within these doors; within this roof / The enemy of all your graces lives' (2. 3. 17–18); 'this house is but a butchery. / Abhor it, fear it, do not enter it' (ll. 27–8).

ORLANDO Why whither Adam would'st thou have me go?
ADAM No matter whither, so you come not here.

(2. 3. 29–30)

Clearly the audience is invited to recognize by these repeated indexical utterances that one of the doors represents the offstage Oliver and his evil intents; the repetition of 'in' marks it as the 'inward' door, which is already (in Act 1) associated with Duke Frederick's abuse of power. There is a staggered exit 'outwards' at the end of this scene: Orlando sets off for the wide world, and Adam has the stage to himself for a moment to farewell his old home and place within the official order, then to make a strongly symbolic exit to follow Orlando 'To the last gasp with truth and loyalty' (2. 3. 69–70). The purpose of this staggered exit becomes clear with the beginning of the next scene, the entrance from 'outwards' of Rosalind and Celia in their new guises, accompanied by Touchstone: Adam's eight lines of rumination are just enough to get Orlando well offstage so that the audience does not have irrelevant thoughts about Rosalind and Celia bumping into him immediately behind the tiring-house wall.

With the arrival of Celia and Rosalind in Arden the audience's reading of the symbolic significance of the two doors takes a subtle shift, which it will retain to the end of the play. The 'inwards' door remains the locus of power, which in this play as we have already seen is associated with the most dominant male – from now on this will be Duke Senior, attended by his retinue of 'loving lords'. We are told that they live in the forest – as outlaws their camp would be *deep* in the forest; the Duke's inner sanctum is his 'cave'.

In opposition to this, the 'outwards' door comes to represent the direction towards the girls' cottage and sheep pasture, 'the skirts of the forest' (3. 2. 329). The onstage space, which is not inhabited by both groups until the last scene of the play, is to be thought of as a space *between* the masculine inner domain and the feminine/working-class outer domain. For the audience, it will automatically constitute one of two spaces, one close to the cottage, one deeper in the woods.

The work of social and topographical historians is helpful in clarifying for today's readers and audiences what would have been natural connotations of certain terms for the Elizabethan audience. This work marks a very recent revision of the standard 'aesthetic' critical judgement that the play operates on a simple country/court opposition based in the literary genre of pastoral, and summarized in the memorable but simplistic opening speech of Duke Senior in Act 2:

Now my co-mates and brothers in exile,
Hath not old custom made this life more sweet
Than that of painted pomp? Are not these woods
More free from peril than the envious court?
.   .   .   .   .   .
Sweet are the uses of adversity
.   .   .   .   .
And this our life, exempt from public haunt,
Finds tongues in trees, books in the running brooks,
Sermons in stones, and good in everything.

(2. 1. 1–17)

The Duke is indulging in the classic Boetian notion of 'the consolations of philosophy': the simple life is enough to satisfy the most thoughtful person, if he (never she!) is wise enough to forego the comforts and pleasures of civilization. The Duke is making the most of his 'exile' – but perhaps he can afford to be so philosophical only because he is supported by a band of courtiers and servants. The actor playing Amiens might well choose to inflect with irony his response to the Duke's somewhat trite speech:

I would not change it. Happy is your Grace,
That can translate the stubbornness of fortune
Into so quiet and so sweet a style.

(2. 1. 18–20)

For the realities of the life of the exiles in the forest mean that the violence which the play has already associated with powerful men is reproduced here: not, perhaps, in so vicious a manner, but unmistakably, via an emphatic image-cluster which an audience would grasp without difficulty on one hearing:

DUKE SENIOR Come, shall we go and kill us venison?
    And yet it irks me the poor dappled fools,
    Being native burghers of this desert city,
    Should in their own confines with forked heads
    Have their round haunches gor'd.
FIRST LORD   Indeed my lord,
    The melancholy Jaques grieves at that,
    And in that kind swears you do more usurp
    Than doth your brother that hath banish'd you.

(2. 1. 21–8)

(Note how the loaded word 'usurp' is placed at the end of a line so that the actor will naturally stress it with a small pause.) Jaques' 'moralizing' of the spectacle of the wounded deer, as reported by the First Lord, presents an alternative image of life in the greenwood from that of the Duke's opening speech, but with equal rhetorical force. In fact the most interesting thing about it is the commentary on it by the First Lord: instead of Amiens' assent (whether ironical or not) to the Duke's clichés, we have a piece of literary criticism which destabilizes the neat binaries of pastoral:

> Thus most invectively he pierceth through
> The body of *country, city, court,*
> Yea, and of this our life, swearing that we
> Are mere usurpers, tyrants, and what's worse,
> To fright the animals and kill them up
> In their assign'd and native dwelling-place.

> (2. 1. 58–63, my emphasis)

Jaques and the First Lord's analysis of the social structure is radical: wherever we are placed in the hierarchy, we are implicated in violence and oppression. The lines constitute a powerful critique of the colonialist impulse which had already gripped Elizabethan England and which Shakespeare was to anatomize so trenchantly in his late play *The Tempest*, where it is again aligned with the desire of the dominant male to retain – and increase – his power.

Thus, by the end of the relatively short scene introducing the 'good' Duke and his co-mates in exile, the audience has been led to associate him rather more closely than a simple binary structure would suggest with his 'evil' brother. Added to this evidence from the dialogue, as I have already suggested, are the visual effects that can be created by doubling the parts of both Dukes, and having them enter through the 'inwards' door, the door of power.

What complicates any simplistic identification between the two authority-figures is the fact that Duke Senior and his companions are outlaws: they have legally no right to be in the forest, which had been the domain of the King since the Norman Conquest. The *OED* under 'forest' gives: '2. *Law*. A woodland district, usually belonging to the king, set apart for

23

hunting wild beasts and game, etc., having its own laws and officers'. Either Duke Senior is claiming his right to kill deer in what is properly his domain, or he is playing at Robin Hood and his Merry Men. He is at once a figure of authority and a figure of revolt. The audience may take it 'as they like it'.

Early in the play Charles the wrestler has told us of the community that Duke Senior has set up in the Forest of Arden, 'like the old Robin Hood of England'. This is a radical, not to say revolutionary image – 'They say many young gentlemen flock to him *every day*' – even if that suggestion is immediately tempered by a safe literary image of unproductive time-wasting – 'and fleet the time carelessly as they did in the golden world' (1. 1. 116–19). For an English audience of the late sixteenth century, which had recently been enjoying a spate of Robin Hood plays,[5] there might well have been a frisson of political radicalism in this reference. There had been angry gatherings against enclosure of common lands in the Midlands; peasants had been deprived of their subsistence properties, and many fled to the forests to set up communities outside the law, poaching game from the royal reserves. 'No Shakespearean text transmits more urgently the imminence of the social breakdown threatened by the conjuncture of famine and enclosure', argues Richard Wilson.[6] 'The Forest of Arden', Stuart Daley points out, was 'a dominant geographical feature of the central Midlands since the Middle Ages[;] by the sixteenth century the Forest or Woodland of Arden had become a famous and storied region covering over two hundred square miles in the heart of England.' But in the 'bitter cold and crop failures of 1596–1598 ... the poor of Warwickshire had suffered grievously in early 1597 and again a year later "for the extreame want and scarsity of graine in that countie, and specially at Stratford uppon Avon, Alcester and other places thereaboutes"' – Shakespeare's home ground.[7] Flight to the Forest of Arden would have been a real option for such once-respectable people.

Such outlaws are romanticized in the play by the transformation of the real Warwickshire Forest of Arden into the literary French locus of Ardenne. A disturbing social reality is replaced by the myth of the dispossessed band of noble men which is characteristic of the Robin Hood stories (Robin is 'Earl of Huntingdon' in the popular plays of 1598). Orlando – of gentle blood, but deprived of his rights as a gentleman – is a natural member of this band of brothers.

Orlando's first encounter with them is a classic dramatic *peripeteia* – 'Forbear, and eat no more!' – as he rushes onto the stage with drawn sword. Having served its purpose of waking up the audience after some rather tedious diatribes from Jaques, the scene goes on to explore further the contradictions that are implict in the Elizabethan idea of masculinity. Orlando's phallic sword-waving interruption draws from the Duke the unaggressive, even pedagogical, response of a man comfortable in his senior status:

> Art thou thus bolden'd man by thy distress?
> Or else a rude despiser of good manners,
> That in civility thou seem'st so empty?

> (2. 7. 92–4)

The binary opposition between *civilization* and *rudeness* or uneducated rusticity is one of the basic issues in the literary genre of pastoral, which acknowledges its unreality in so far as its shepherds are apparently natural composers of sophisticated verses who have nothing better to do with their time (I discuss this theme further in chapter 5). But the Duke and his co-mates and brothers in exile present a more complex image than this literary cliché, since they are, by virtue of their class, civilized. Yet, as Orlando says, the expectation created by their being in the forest is that

> I thought that all things had been savage here,
> And therefore put I on the countenance
> Of stern commandment.

> (2. 7. 107–9)

That is, therefore *he* played the role of dominant male. The result of this assumption's being disrupted is that Orlando changes his self-presentation, moving radically from the opening visual image of the aggressive warrior, sword in hand, with his imperious demands, to a rhetorical image of himself as nurturing and feminine-maternal:

> Then but forbear your food a little while,
> Whiles, like a doe, I go to find my fawn,
> And give it food.

> (2. 7. 127–9)

25

What I have called the destabilizing of Orlando's ideological assumptions takes place through a longer, almost hypnotic, exchange of verbal formulas about a *past* golden age, when the hierarchy of patriarchal governance guaranteed good order in the community, as opposed to the violent disorder that we saw in Act 1:

ORLANDO .   .   .   .
    If ever you have look'd on better days,
    If ever been where bells have knoll'd to church,
    If ever sat at any good man's feast,
    If ever from your eyelids wiped a tear
    And know what 'tis to pity and be pitied,
    Let gentleness my strong enforcement be:
    In the which hope I blush, and hide my sword.
DUKE SENIOR True is it that we have seen better days,
    And have with holy bell been knoll'd to church
    And sat at good men's feasts and wiped our eyes
    Of drops that sacred pity hath engender'd:
    And therefore sit you down in gentleness
    And take upon command what help we have
    That to your wanting may be minister'd.

(2. 7. 113–26)

The effect of this repetition is to call up an image of the once *and future* benevolent patriarchy, which will include the 'nurture' of femininity (providing food, weeping with 'sacred pity'). There is a soothing nostalgia here, which guarantees that the threat of genuine social rebellion will not be carried out. The Duke and his band of exiles do not follow the Robin Hood model: they do not go about righting wrongs, robbing from the rich to give to the poor, challenging corrupt authority: they leave the mechanism of the literary romance plot to bring about justice and the restoration of order, while they enjoy their games in Never Land. The play, by remaining within the literary genre of the pastoral, defuses its own potential political radicalism – and, indeed, converts it back into a safe conservatism. The social order at the end of the play is unchanged, though the embodiments of authority and power (Duke Senior and his heir-elect, Orlando) are undoubtedly more benign than those who had usurped it at the play's beginning.

Nevertheless, and for all the Duke's claims to have created in

26

the forest an ideal civil society, the play insists on our continuing to notice how implicated Duke Senior is in the violence he apparently rejects. While this scene works hard to establish a benign image of the Duke's utopian community, both 2. 1 (as we have already noted) and the only other 'forest' scene, the brief 4. 2, stress that the iconically masculine pursuit of hunting is the band's major entertainment when not sitting around philosophizing. (Significantly enough the picnic in 2. 5 appears to consist of 'fruit', not meat.) Act 4 scene 2 seems to have no other purpose than, late in the play's games with pastoralism, to remind the audience of this ideology of *machismo*: opening with Jaques' question to his co-mates, 'Which is he that killed the deer?', it is the opportunity for a hearty song with chorus celebrating the chief killer. But typically for this play, the moment contains its own deconstruction. The song's second half swings gleefully to the uncomfortable downside of phallocentrism, the condition of the never-ending competition between males:

> *Take thou no scorn to wear the horn,*
> *It was a crest ere thou wast born,*
> *Thy father's father wore it,*
> *And thy father bore it.*
> *The horn, the horn, the lusty horn,*
> *Is not a thing to laugh to scorn.*

> (4. 2. 10–19)

The deer's horn is *either* the sign of phallic triumph, *or* the sign of being cuckolded by a more powerful male – and no man can ever be certain under what sign he is (seen to be) performing.

Hunting, then, via a few striking images, both verbal and visual, symbolizes in the play's forest scenes the violent and competitive ideology of masculinity which we saw in the more conventionally narrative first act of the play. The 'narrative' of Acts 2–5 of the play is largely to do with courtship leading to multiple weddings, which we shall examine in later chapters, but it is worth noting that both Rosalind and Orlando, the play's principal lovers, begin their adventures in the forest disguised as hunters, that is, dressed iconically as unambiguously masculine. Rosalind's plan for her disguise is specific, and the lines suggest that she is quite excited about such a radical gender-switch:

27

> Were it not better,
> Because that I am more than common tall,
> That I did suit me *all points like a man*?
> A gallant curtle-axe upon my thigh,
> A boar-spear in my hand . . .
>
> (1. 3. 110–14, my emphasis)

Note the doubly phallic weaponry – all points like a man, indeed! But once she is established in the cottage 'on the skirts of the forest' she is identified as a 'young shepherd', a totally non-aggressive image, and we can assume that the actor of the role will have left off carrying her weapons after 2. 4.

Orlando not only displays his masculine aggression in 2. 7, but we are also told in 3. 2 that he has the appearance of a 'forester' (l. 292) – as he would have as a member of the Duke's band – and that he 'was furnished like a hunter' (l. 241). 'O ominous!' cries Rosalind, 'he comes to kill my heart!' – signalling via a pun what we are about to see, the transformation of Orlando from male-oriented hunter/forester to pastoral courtly lover whose principal weapon is language (even if ridiculously inscribed on the barks of trees). And, as we shall see in the courtship scenes, in accepting the sexually ambiguous courtship of a 'Ganymede' Orlando has distanced himself temporarily from the repressed homophobia of the (homosocial) band of outlaws.

'LIKE FRINGE UPON A PETTICOAT'

If the Duke and his merry men live deep in the 'woody parts' of the Forest of Arden – and the Duke, as most powerful man of this community, has an inner sanctum in his 'cave' – Rosalind and Celia are clearly imagined as inhabiting a different part of the forest, the 'fruitfull pastures' or small pastoral holdings between the deep woods and the manorial lands and villages outside the forest. Stuart Daley points out that 'grazing was a principal land use of [Elizabethan] forests, and sheep husbandry a widespread Tudor industry'.[8] There are plenty of clues to this imagined topography in the play, which contrasts with the hunting imagery associated with the deep woods.

At their first meeting Rosalind replies to Orlando's question, 'Where dwell you, pretty youth?' with the telling simile, 'With this shepherdess my sister; here in the skirts of the forest, like fringe upon a petticoat' (3. 2. 328–30). Their offstage space is gendered feminine, not only because the women live there, but also because it is a *liminal* area, suitable for 'boys and women' who have yet to attain a fixed position in relation to male power (the boys by becoming men, the women by marrying). The feminine metaphor is later reiterated via Oliver's request 'Where in the purlieus of this forest stands/A sheep-cote fenc'd about with olive-trees?' (4. 3. 76–7): a purlieu is 'a piece or tract of land on the fringe or border of a forest' (*OED*). It is also a place where the principal activity is the non-violent grazing and shearing of sheep. Interestingly, before the girls' arrival in the forest, the sheepcote had fallen into desuetude because it was the property of an absent and unconcerned landlord:

> CORIN ...I am shepherd to another man
> And do not shear the fleeces that I graze.
> My master is of churlish disposition,
> And little recks to find the way to heaven
> By doing deeds of hospitality.
> Besides, his cote, his flocks, and bounds of feed
> Are now on sale, and at our sheepcote now,
> By reason of his absence, there is nothing
> That you will feed on.
>
> (2. 4. 76–83)

When Celia buys the place, not only is she embodying in the stage-play world the radical notion that women should be free to own and work property, she is also proposing a kinder, gentler capitalism: 'we will mend thy wages' (l. 92). The girls are literally creating a 'women's space' which has more autonomy than the always-vulnerable private space that we saw in Act 1. It is enclosed – 'a sheep-cote fenc'd about with olive-trees' – a safe, walled Eden-like place – and it is in a 'bottom', which as Daley points out is 'a term of English husbandry meaning a water meadow or fat pasture land in a valley, where woods would not be tolerated'.[9] It is a recognizably feminine topographical feature as opposed to the phallic stands of trees of the deep woods.

Both these offstage spaces are of course only imaginary, but as I have demonstrated (following Daley), they are clearly and consistently differentiated in the text of the play, with verbal signals that would have been easier for an Elizabethan audience

29

to pick up than is the case with modern audiences ignorant of agricultural practices. Furthermore, we are usually presented with a stage fully dressed with trees – but as Daley rightly asserts, 'The notion of a leaf-smothered Arden is an anachronistic romantic invention'. Daley further makes the point that 'To Phebe, Orlando, and Duke Senior, Ganymede is manifestly a shepherd youth...and whoever wants to see the youth – whether Orlando, Phebe, Silvius, or Oliver – must come to the sheep farm...for that is her venue'.[10] Thus the 'empty space' which is the Elizabethan stage, in the scenes involving Rosalind and Celia, is imagined as 'hard by' their sheep-cote and cottage. It is a different empty space from that inhabited by the foresters, with its 'brook that brawls along this wood' (2. 1. 32) to which a deer wounded in the hunt might run.

One further topographical clue remains to be examined. When Celia responds to Oliver's request for directions in 4. 3, she gives the information that the sheep-cote is 'West of this place' (l. 78). If we map this direction onto the physical reality of the theatre in which the words were probably first heard – and we must imagine that a gesture would accompany them (everyone points when asked directions) – then Celia would point unambiguously to the stage-left door of the Globe stage (which was oriented to face north-east). To an audience accustomed to reading its directions from the sun it would be unnecessarily productive of jeers to be anything other than literally accurate here. This means that we can identify the 'outwards' door associated with women and the powerless as the south-west or stage-left door; the 'inwards', male-associated door with stage right. This disposition confirms the long-held theatrical tradition that a stage-right entry is the most powerful. That is, Shakespeare's internal stage directions are devised so as to reinforce the audience's symbolic reading of the stage space and its imagined offstage areas.[11]

We might take this insight a little further, though here I am being speculative and basing an argument merely on the chimings of certain words in the text which are themselves metaphors and have no reference to verifiable historical reality, apart from the devious history of the English language. When Orlando first bursts in on the Duke and his picnic party and then has to apologize for his rude behaviour, he says 'Yet am I *inland* bred,/And know some nurture' (2. 7. 97–8, my emphasis). The Arden editor glosses this as 'not rustic and awkward', and invites us to compare it with a later passage, in which Rosalind/Ganymede explains her refined accent by reference to 'an old religious uncle of mine...who was in his youth an *inland* man, one that knew courtship too well' (3. 2. 335–8). Madeline Doran explicates this with the help of dictionaries both ancient and modern:

> The *OED* glosses *inland* in this passage as 'having the refinement characteristic of the inlying districts of a country.' Shakespeare himself makes both the literal and the derivative sense abundantly clear, for *removed* is the opposite of *inland*, and *courtship* means 'the ways of the court' as well as 'courting' in love.[12]

Shakespeare seems to have invented the epithet 'inland'; these two passages are the only *OED* citations, and Doran remarks in a footnote: '*Upland* and *uplandish* are common in sixteenth-century dictionaries; *outland* and *outlandish* are occasional; *inland* I nowhere found'. Doran continues,

> To return to our 'inland' man, of whom civil behaviour is expected. It would help us to know why Shakespeare used just this epithet if we were given an equivalent term for his opposite, the man who is expected to be rude. Our natural impulse is to supply 'outland man'. But *outland* and *outlandish* were commonly used in the sense of 'foreign' or 'strange', not implied here; the words did not necessarily connote 'barbarous' in the sense of 'savage'. A 'borderer', then?...A rustic, perhaps, or 'uplandish' man?...Indeed, the charge Orlando makes against his elder brother is that Oliver keeps him, unlike his brother Jaques, who is at school, 'rustically at home'....
>
> All these implications – remoteness from city or court, barbarousness, wildness, lack of education, rusticity – are present in what the 'inland' man is not. 'Removedness' from civil society (and all that that implies) seems to be the condition all these senses have in common.[13]

Doran goes on to argue that Shakespeare is on neither one side nor the other in the arguments about the civilized versus the rustic life. My point, however, is that there is a metaphorical chain here to which we might add one more link: that the status and power embodied in the utopian ideal of civilization is literally both represented and its claims to moral superiority deconstructed by the stage's association of 'inwards' with

31

corrupt masculine power. In short, it is better, and morally more honest, to live 'in the skirts of the forest', to be a borderer, a liminal figure, a woman, adolescent male or labourer. Further, to return to Steven Mullaney's description of the theatre's place in the 'Liberties' of London and our notion of the phenomenology of the gaze, we might speculate that the audience is already positioned to look with more empathy on – to feel themselves represented by – those actors associated with the 'outwards', stage-left space. Drama, Mullaney argues,

> is the literary art of space, virtual or otherwise; it is the art that most concretely employs distance – literal, aesthetic, ideological, and historical – to bring reigning ideologies and cultural climates into view...[14]

The action that originates from the stage-left door is more likely to be exploratory, disruptive, defiant of authority and 'reigning ideology'. It represents the liminality of the theatre and the experience it offers. And although it is the condition of liminality to be always only temporary, a moment between, or time out ('there's no clock in the forest', 3. 2. 295), 'strange things', as Rosalind says (5. 2. 59), magic, can be done in that space. The most remarkable is the deconstructive play with gender, sexuality, and the traditions of courtship that is the main business of the character of Rosalind/Ganymede.

4

Call Me Ganymede

Few critical issues in Shakespearean comedy have been discussed more energetically in the last twenty years than the question of what it meant to an Elizabethan audience to see boys playing the roles of women. For modern play-goers it is largely a dead issue (though I shall discuss in chapter 7 some late-twentieth-century productions which attempted to explore the potential of all-male casts); since the mid-seventeenth century the roles of Rosalind and Celia, Phebe and Audrey, have been claimed as their right by actresses who revel in the richness of Shakespeare's language and the potential for complex explorations of gender and sexuality that the roles allow.

There is an important distinction to be made here in the ideas about what it is that the actor/actress does on stage: do they impersonate the character or do they imitate it, standing apart from it a little so that we can see the gap between the actor and the role? Modern Western actors, for the most part, are locked into an ideology of 'becoming' the character, an ideology based on the dominance of naturalism in twentieth-century theatre, and particularly on the claim of films to represent 'reality' and therefore to demand total immersion of actors in the roles they are performing. This was not the theory in Elizabethan theatre, though throughout the history of Western theatre we find audiences praising actors for their 'natural' representation of characters. (A glance at any fifty-year-old film, however, will demonstrate that the criteria of 'natural' acting change approximately every half-century.)

Elizabethan theatre and acting delighted in the conscious recognition of its own artificiality. Disguise, masks, the performance of plays within plays, and word-play by characters on the notions of acting and theatre, are some of the means by which

33

this consciousness was never allowed to lapse. Moreover, the plays that were performed on Shakespeare's stage almost never purported to represent contemporary life: their worlds were distant in time and place. Further, the characters spoke in blank verse most of the time – an artificially heightened version of the English language that allowed rich use of metaphor and other poetic devices that gave pleasure to audience and readers. (*As You Like It* has Jaques remind the audience of just this convention of artificiality: 'Nay then God buy you, and you talk in blank verse!' (4. 1. 29) – ironically enough, in response to Orlando's natural-sounding 'Good day and happiness, dear Rosalind'.)

Nevertheless, C. L. Barber, in the seminal work *Shakespeare's Festive Comedy* (1959) observed that Shakespeare

> wrote at a moment when the educated part of society was modifying a ceremonial, ritualistic conception of human life to create a historical, psychological conception. His drama, indeed, was an important agency in this transformation: it provided a 'theater' where the failures of ceremony could be looked at in a place apart and understood as history; it provided new ways of representing relations between language and action so as to express personality...his comedy presents holiday magic as imagination, games as expressive gestures.[1]

I shall explore the idea of Shakespeare's injection of 'personality' into roles for actors later in this chapter by comparison with Lodge's originary text *Rosalynd*. Perhaps the vexed notion of 'naturalism' can be laid to rest with the formulation that Shakespeare's lines and scenes – despite their poetic artifice and witty conceits – are rich and complex enough for actors to apply their culture's notion of psychology to the characters. There is enough in the lines that actors can make sense of; they can fill in the missing bits of their narratives to create an illusion for the audience of meaningful human behaviour.

Whereas in the tragedies Shakespeare helps the actor create this illusion by providing him with soliloquies in which he explains himself to the audience (thereby, paradoxically, breaking a simple illusion of naturalism, the 'fourth wall' convention), in *As You Like It* there are no soliloquies. 'What is missing', says Karen Newman, is not a sense of [Rosalind's] inner life or personal struggles...but rather self-consciousness about that equipoise expressed through soliloquy. Rosalind's inner debates are externalized in her role as Ganymede/Rosalind, and we are correspondingly distanced from her feelings, however much we may appreciate her character. We share the pleasures of flirtations, of transvestism, of shifting roles and playful irony, all of which testify to Rosalind's fascination by giving her dimensions in excess of her function. We are called upon to hold together, in the study or in performance, the multiple aspects of her character, but we never have the sense that she herself recognizes or struggles with that multiplicity.[2]

This seems to me a helpful formulation of a tricky issue. Rosalind, in her highly theatrical role as girl-playing-boy-playing-girl, is clearly a *performative* character: her role is to embody and make available to the audience the performative nature of those 'natural' categories we take for granted, such as gender. And here, if we wish, we can take into consideration the historical fact that this immensely playable and therefore believable character was originally performed by a boy (as were also, of course, Celia, Audrey, and Phebe). Michael Shapiro suggests of the original performances of the play,

On Shakespeare's stage, these oscillations [between female and male identity] became even more dazzling in the light of the spectators' dual consciousness of the boy actor producing all of these abrupt shifts. These multiple layers of identity and the swift movements from one to another produced a theatrical vibrancy that engaged audiences in the illusion that an amalgam constructed of multiple and discrete layers of identity represented a unified character.[3]

The notion of a 'unified character' might well be an anachronism, as I suggested above, but Shapiro does point to one of the particular pleasures that the play provides: the Elizabethan theatre's liminal space is here utilized to disrupt fixed notions of gender through a safe and pleasurable spectacle: the boy who plays the girl (who, in this play, even more disruptively, plays the boy who plays the girl).

Much recent scholarship has attempted to tease out, through the reading of other contemporary documents, just what were the erotic and sexual politics of this experience for that original audience.[4] Was it a homoerotic stage? that is, was the pleasure of the audience in watching the representation of the heterosexual lovemaking in fact a much more subversive pleasure in watching a man and a boy make love? Undoubtedly in *As You Like It* the audience was aware of the *double entendre* in Rosalind's decision to take as her male name 'no worse a name than Jove's own page,/And therefore look you call me Ganymede' (1. 3. 120–21) – since 'Ganymede' was a slang term for a young male homosexual. But, as Stephen Orgel argues, 'there is no indication whatever that Shakespeare is doing something sexually daring there, skating on thin ice'.[5] He presents evidence that the love of Elizabethan men for boys was generally unproblematic in that culture, rendered acceptable by the many literary models in Ovid and other ancient texts; and, in fact, often thought of as less dangerous than love for women, whose sexuality was thought to be voraciously over-whelming, effeminizing of 'manly' men. Although the puritans fulminated against the theatre in general, the potential for homosexual behaviour was only one aspect of their larger phobia. It was basically 'the universal sexuality evoked by theatre, a lust not distinguished by the gender of its object'[6] which was unacceptable to puritans – especially as it disrupts the specific definitions of gender and sexuality which are the bedrock of the patriarchal system. Even more so when in a play such as *As You Like It* such issues are amusingly foregrounded.

Yet on another level, as Orgel points out, the transvestite theatre simply reproduces the order of patriarchy. For 'boys and women are for the most part cattle of this colour' (3. 2. 402–3). 'Cattle' – Rosalind's slang puns significantly: the word is cognate with 'chattel', household possession. The boys were apprentices (not to theatre guilds, but to any profession convenient):[7] dependant and 'a medium of exchange within the patriarchal structure, and both [women and boys] are (perhaps in consequence) constructed as objects of erotic attraction to adult men'.[8] Orgel's conclusion to the interesting question, 'Why did only boys play women?' – or why the transvestite stage was so unproblematically homoerotic – is that

> eroticized boys appear to be a middle term between men and women, and far from precluding the love of women, they are represented as *enabling* figures, as a way of getting from men to women.... In a society that has an investment in seeing women as imperfect men, the danger points will be those at which women

reveal that they have an independent essence, an existence that is not, in fact, under male control, a power and authority that either challenges male authority, or, more dangerously, that is not simply a version or parody of maleness, but is specifically female....In this context Rosalind's male disguise would be, in the deepest sense, for Orlando's benefit, not for Rosalind's; it would constitute a way around the dangers of the female libido.[9]

Orgel's scholarly speculations are an exciting insight into certain Elizabethan discursive fields which operate largely at the level of unconscious assumptions. On the other hand, historians such as Kathleen McLuskie and Jean Howard argue that at some level boy actors playing women must simply have been accepted in performance as a convention.[10] Otherwise, there would have been little audience involvement with those aspects of the plays based on the representation of heterosexual desire. Howard goes on to underline the equally discursive nature of this more overt representation:

> The representation of Rosalind's holiday humour has the primary effect, I think, of confirming the gender system and perfecting rather than dismantling it by making a space of mutuality within relations of dominance.... Progressively this text has narrowed the range of erotic possibilities the play has mobilized in the direction of heterosexual coupling. For example, it has displaced the same-sex bonds between Rosalind and Celia with heterosexual unions; it has muted the homoerotic implications of Rosalind's assumption of the name Ganymede by having Rosalind and Orlando so firmly committed to the heterosexual other; and, as with Olivia, it has corrected Phebe's 'mistake' in loving a man who is 'really' a woman.[11]

If we take the evidence of the play's *telos*, its drive towards closure, then, we will conclude that the play privileges a heterosexual interpretation of the energy flow between adult male actor and adolescent boy-as-woman. But this is somewhat to oversimplify the experience of the audience in the theatre – that liminal space where anything may happen – particularly its moment-by-moment awareness of the potential for disruption that the cross-dressing generates. (It is also to ignore the astonishing Epilogue to this play, on which I shall comment later.)

Two critics who have opened up the possibilities for discussion of what might have been the phenomenological experience of the audience watching the performance of this story are Valerie Traub and Stephen Greenblatt. Traub argues, incisively:

> Clearly, insofar as gender hierarchies seem to be both temporarily transgressed *and* formally reinstated, the question of subversion versus containment can only be resolved by crediting *either* the expense of dramatic energy *or* comedic closure. Yet, to do either is also to reproduce the artificial distinction between content and form – a capitulation to the logic of binarism.[12]

Traub's version of 'the homoeroticism of *As You Like It*' identifies it as

> playful in its ability to transcend binary oppositions, to break into a dual mode, a simultaneity, of desire. Insofar as Rosalind/Ganymede is a multiple sexual object (simultaneously heterosexual and homoerotic), Orlando's effusion of desire toward him/her prevents the stable reinstitution of heterosexuality, upon which the marriage plot depends...
>
> In excess of the dominant ideology of monogamous heterosexuality, to which Rosalind is symbolically wed at the end of the play, exist desires unsanctioned by institutional favor. By means of her male improvisation, Rosalind leads the play into a mode of desire neither heterosexual nor homoerotic, but both heterosexual *and* homoerotic. As much as she displays her desire for Orlando, she also enjoys her position as male object of Phebe's desire and, more importantly, of Orlando's.[13]

Traub here, I think, touches on the simple reason for the play's apparent formal weakness. Earlier critics argued that it lacks drive, it lacks plot, its lacks motivation. Nevertheless, it is infinitely delightful because of the charm of Rosalind. But in what does this charm consist? Wit and vitality undoubtedly: but most audience members, when quizzed, would locate the play's charm in the courtship scenes. And these scenes are perpetually delightful because of the 'multiple erotic possibilities and positions' that they offer through a cheekily self-conscious employment of the dramatic 'if' – Touchstone's 'If you said so, then I said so' (5. 4. 100–101): 'The dependence on the conditional structures the possibility of erotic exploration without necessitating a commitment to it'.[14]

Stephen Greenblatt's essay 'Fiction and Friction' offers an analysis of Renaissance theories about sexual anatomy as a way of entering into an understanding of the multiple eroticism of

38

Shakespearean comedy. In brief, the view of these anatomists is that women's sexual organs are the same as men's, only hidden and inverted inside the body. For generation to occur, there must be a pleasant 'chafing', which will cause the hidden female 'penis' to ejaculate. Shakespeare realized, argues Greenblatt,

> that if sexual chafing could not be presented literally onstage, it could be represented figuratively: friction could be fictionalized, chafing chastened and hence made fit for the stage, by transforming it into the witty, erotically charged sparring that is the heart of the lovers' experience.
>
> By means of this transformation Shakespeare invested his comedies with a powerful sexual commotion, a collective excitation, an imaginative heat that the plots promise will be realized offstage, in the marriage beds towards which they gesture.... the unrepresented consummations of unrepresented marriages call attention to the unmooring of desire, the generalizing of the libidinal, that is the special pleasure of Shakespearean fiction. For the representation of chafing is not restricted to Shakespeare's lovers; it is diffused throughout the comedies as a system of foreplay.

'Moreover,' Greenblatt continues,

> for Shakespeare friction is specifically associated with verbal wit; indeed at moments the plays seem to imply that erotic friction *originates* in the wantonness of language and thus that the body itself is a tissue of metaphors or, conversely, that language is perfectly embodied.... Dallying with words is the principal Shakespearean representation of erotic heat.[15]

In the second part of this chapter I shall explore this insight in relation to the courtship scenes in *As You Like It*, proceeding by comparison with the parallel scenes in the originary text, Thomas Lodge's *Rosalynd*.

DALLYING WITH WORDS

Shakespeare's Act 3 scene 2 and Act 4 scene 1 – the courtship scenes in the forest between Rosalind (disguised as Ganymede), Celia, and Orlando – are modelled on two segments of Lodge's 1590 novel. Looking at the Lodge text, it quickly becomes clear that the major change that Shakespeare made was in reducing the 'literariness' of Lodge's writing (Lodge's text is subtitled

'Euphues' Golden Legacy', in deliberate homage to the fashion-able work of John Lyly). Lodge's Orlando (confusingly known as Rosader) performs five 'sonnetos' and a shared eclogue in the course of the courtship scenes: in Shakespeare these are represented by a couple of parodic pieces, read by the girls and improvised on by Touchstone. Rosader is generally more eloquent than Orlando – better educated and more consciously genteel. As performer of his own poems, he is given more textual space than Orlando; he is the 'hero' of the narrative much more than Rosalynd is the 'heroine'.

A duetting eclogue is the only moment in Lodge when 'Ganymede' offers to 'represent Rosalynd', her eloquence matching Rosader's in a highly formal versified lovers' debate; there is no offer of a 'cure' through an extended cross-gender game as there is in Shakespeare, though Lodge's Ganymede does offer plenty of advice to Rosader about giving up the self-indulgent pains of love. She is eloquent but not witty in the way that Shakespeare's Rosalind is; her intelligence is displayed more through her performance of florid euphuistic prose and elaborate classical references. (The Silvius and Phebe scenes of Shakespeare are a comic displacement of the earnest pastoral of Lodge's principal characters; see discussion in chapter 5.) Lodge was apparently not interested in the comic or sexual potential of Rosalynd's cross-dressing; for him, safely in a disembodied novel, the girl-as-page trope is simply a plot device. Celia/Aliena has rather more to say in Lodge than in Shakespeare, though the mock marriage which is the culmination of both 'wooings' is over very quickly in Lodge, with none of the anxiety with which Shakespeare surrounds this doubly transgressive act (I discuss this in chapter 6).

Shakespeare transformed the text he had at his elbow into a brilliantly playable theatre script which built on the expertise (and ambivalence) of his boy-players of female parts. This transformation is of the order of a quantum leap. But the experiment of workshopping the Lodge text[16] indicates that had Shakespeare not decided to work his professional magic on this novel, it could still have made a perfectly respectable popular play of the 1590s, in the pastoral romance mode.

The first scene in Lodge which is closely equivalent to Shakespeare (3. 2) is the one in which we first hear Rosader/

Orlando's poems. They are not nearly as dire as 'From the east to western Inde', but they do have the same persistent repetitiveness:

> Of all chaste birds the Phoenix doth excel,
> Of all strong beasts the lion bears the bell,
> Of all sweet flowers the rose doth sweetest smell,
> Of all fair maids my Rosalynd is fairest.
>
> Of all pure metals gold is only purest,
> Of all high trees the pine hath highest crest,
> Of all soft sweets I like my mistress' breast,
> Of all chaste thoughts my mistress' thoughts are rarest. (etc.)[17]

The conversation between Rosader, Rosalynd and Aliena which follows this effusion is led by Rosalynd as Ganymede in a style very similar to Shakespeare's Rosalind, a hearty parade of manliness which would not fool anyone less self-absorbed: 'What news, forester? hast thou wounded some deer, and lost him in the fall? Care not man for so small a loss' (R. 68). And although the scene does not lead to a proposed 'love-cure', it is led by Rosalynd onto not dissimilar erotic ground, as she encourages Rosader thus: 'Much have I heard of thy mistress' excellence, and I know, forester, thou canst describe her at the full, as one that hast surveyed all her parts with a curious eye; then do me that favour, to tell me what her perfections be' (R. 69). This is of course a cue for a blazon, a nine-stanza feature-by-feature description of Rosalynd's physical excellences: it includes such amorous fantasies as:

> Her paps are centres of delight,
> Her paps are orbs of heavenly frame,
> Where nature moulds the dew of light,
> To feed perfection with the same:
> Heigh ho, would she were mine.
>
> With orient pearl, with ruby red,
> With marble white, with sapphire blue,
> Her body every way is fed;
> Yet soft in touch, and sweet in view . . .
>
> (R. 70)

It is only after this emphatic reminder of Rosalynd's female body that Lodge toys momentarily with the pleasures provided by the cross-dressing trope: 'It makes me blush', says Rosalynd, 'to hear how women should be so excellent, and pages so unperfect'. Rosader replies that the 'page' 'resembl[es] the shadow' of a woman, to which Rosalynd retorts (after a tart remark by Aliena), 'Who knows not . . . if boys might put on their garments, perhaps they would prove as comely; if not as comely, it may be more courteous' (*R.* 71). Lodge seems to accept the Elizabethan idea that there is little difference between boys and women, and that gender is often simply defined by appearance. The conversation ends with a teasing request from Ganymede for 'more sonnets in commendation of thy mistress', and a promise that Rosader will return tomorrow with more of his literary efforts. The courtship, that is to say, will continue to be conducted through the medium of literature, with Rosader as the male entitled to parade his charms through the use of literary (i.e. educated) forms, and Rosalynd playing the role of the (feminine) respondent, though her male disguise enables her to take on a teasing tone.

For Shakespeare, on the other hand, Orlando's literary affectations are merely a starting point for a much more equal dialogue. It is in fact Rosalind/Ganymede who consciously sets up a display of witty and imaginative verbal facility to Orlando's 'straight man' in their opening dialogue. Orlando feeds the cues to Ganymede: 'Who ambles Time withal? . . . Who doth he gallop withal?' and so on. It's a sort of intellectual flirtation – or friction, to use Greenblatt's term – in which Rosalind/Ganymede claims the ground which is culturally ascribed to the male, abstract reasoning.

Much critical ink has been spent on delving into the significance of Rosalind's disquisition upon Time (3. 2. 302–27): can it be read as a structuring theme of the play? Obviously it has connections with Jaques' 'Seven ages of man' speech (2. 7. 139–66): it reminds us that we all live in Time, and that our perspective on it is dependent on the social role we are playing. But perhaps the most immediately relevant effect is that of subconsciously alerting the audience to the 'time out' or 'holiday' aspect of life in Arden: although it is a place of labour for the shepherds, for the aristocratic visitors it is *not* the 'working-day world' whose 'briers' Rosalind complains about in Act 1. None of the activities and social roles that Rosalind mentions in this dialogue are to be seen in the forest community; as Orlando points out, 'there's no clock in the forest'. Instead a simpler pastoral life, based on broader 'time[s] o' day' (morning, noon, afternoon, night) is to be observed. In due course, the aristocrats who categorize and hierarchize the world of money and status will return to that clock-time.

Modern actors use this sequence, however, for its performative possibilities, not to spell out a sermon to the audience (the same is true of Jaques' famous speech): its function is to charm, even hypnotize, Orlando, so that he will be drawn into the next stage of the courtship – asking for the boy's/girl's address: 'Where dwell you pretty youth?' (3. 2. 328). Rosalind answers in terms that foreground the relation between gender and costume – 'here in the skirts of the forest, like fringe upon a petticoat' (this is often accompanied in the theatre with a hastily covered-up gesture towards the non-existent feminine garment). She goes on to introduce a discussion of femininity as an abstract category: 'I thank God I am not a woman, to be touched with so many giddy offences' (3. 2. 340–4) – so that she can then proceed to deconstruct the Petrarchan stereotype of the 'man in love' (3. 2. 360):

ORLANDO What were his marks?
ROSALIND A lean cheek, which you have not; a blue eye and sunken, which you have not; an unquestionable spirit, which you have not; a beard neglected, which you have not – but I pardon you for that, for simply your having in beard is a younger brother's revenue. Then your hose should be ungartered, your bonnet unbanded, your sleeves unbuttoned, your shoe untied, and everything about you demonstrating a careless desolation. (3. 2. 362–71)

Orlando, despite his literary poses, is pre-eminently, as this speech makes clear to us, a healthy and natural-looking young man: he is not caught up in the conventional discourses of courtly love. Rosalind cannot resist teasing him about this – 'But you are no such man; you are rather point-device in your accoutrements, as loving yourself than seeming the lover of any other' (371–4). Orlando's vitality and self-confidence are an important aspect of his characterization, if he is not to slip from one stereotype – the aggressive young man who protests with his fists – to another, the effeminized lover, whose improper costuming signals him as being 'careless' of his social role as a male. Like Rosalind, although less obviously to modern audiences, Orlando operates outside the strict gender binaries of his society's official discourse.

This point is made more clear by the willingness with which Orlando enters into the love-cure game that Rosalind/Ganymede proposes at the climax of this first courtship scene. Her long speech about her (invented) previous pretence to be a woman provides the equivalent stereotype to the male lover's behaviour that she has just described. The speech becomes obviously parodic through accumulation and exaggeration:

> I set him every day to woo me: at which time would I, being but a moonish youth, grieve, be effeminate, changeable, longing and liking, proud, fantastical, apish, shallow, inconstant, full of tears, full of smiles, for every passion something and for no passion truly anything, as boys and women are for the most part cattle of this colour... (3. 2. 396–403)

Despite this unattractive image, culminating in 'a nook merely monastic', Orlando hesitates only briefly before agreeing to be thus 'cured'. How can the actor justify this decision? The answer must once again lie in the hypnotic energy of Rosalind's words and presence – Orlando wants more of them, on whatever terms. It is interesting, however, to consider the intonations and emphases possible for the actor in his immediate response to Rosalind's speech: 'I would not be cured, youth'. Varieties of resistance, doubt, and self-confidence can be conveyed in these readings of the line:

I would not be cured, youth.

I *would* not be cured, youth.

I would *not* be cured, youth.

I would not *be* cured, youth.

I would not be *cured*, youth.

Rosalind's response – 'I would cure you' – is similarly variable and obviously dependent on the emphasis that Orlando gives his line. But she has an extra weapon up her sleeve, an extra clause, '*if* you would but call me Rosalind and come every day to my cote to woo me'. There is 'much virtue in If', as Touchstone remarks later in the play (5. 4. 102). What Ganymede offers is a new type of imaginative erotics, much more lively and unpredictable than the conventions of literary love-songs; here Orlando can act out his fantasies and perhaps even his frustrated longings through the complex reality created by bodily presence.

The second courtship scene, 4. 1, also has its parallel in Lodge. The changes that Shakespeare made to the text at his elbow are again subtle and significant. This is a much longer scene, culminating in the wooing eclogue and the mock-wedding. It takes place on the following day: Lodge informs us that Ganymede/Rosalynd has had a poor night's sleep, Aliena is feeling very chirpy. The two of them come upon their 'melancholy forester' (who hasn't had a good night's sleep in weeks) and Rosalynd accosts him:

> what makes you so early abroad this morn? In contemplation, no doubt, of your Rosalynd. Take heed, forester; step not too far, the ford may be deep, and you slip over the shoes....'Tis good, forester, to love, but not to overlove, lest in loving her that likes not thee, thou fold thyself in an endless labyrinth. (R. 74)

It is an eloquent warning against the excesses of romantic love which bespeaks the good sense of Lodge's Rosalynd, a trait carried over into Shakespeare's character; but Shakespeare's Orlando, as we have already seen, is certainly not one for moping around. In fact he arrives late for his appointment, having been, we assume, occupied with strengthening his bonds with Duke Senior and his merry men. This tardiness spurs Rosalind to another flight of fancy that carries a sting:

> ROSALIND Nay, and you be so tardy, come no more in my sight. I had as lief be wooed of a snail.
>
> ORLANDO Of a snail?
>
> ROSALIND Ay, of a snail. For though he comes slowly, he carries his house on his head; a better jointure, I think, than you make a woman. Besides, he brings his destiny with him.
>
> ORLANDO What's that?
>
> ROSALIND Why, horns – which such as you are fain to be beholding to your wives for: but he comes armed in his fortune, and prevents the slander of his wife.
>
> (4. 1. 49–59)

A double insult: snails are but lowly (and slimy) creatures hardly to be compared with men, the lords of creation; and yet, they do

45

have something in common with men: 'horns', the sign of cuckoldom. We are reminded subliminally of the play's ongoing deconstruction of the signifiers of masculinity, a theme to be taken up graphically in the following scene, the dance and song of the apparently triumphant hunters.

Lodge, who is not at this point using the Ganymede-as-Rosalynd trope, enables Ganymede to regain her witty defensive control of the situation in a speech in which she seems to want to push Aliena into Rosader's arms ('one bird in the hand is worth two in the wood', R. 74). The opportunity being declined, Rosalynd changes the subject in order to hear more of her lover's praise of her idealized self: 'But leaving this prattle, now I'll put you in mind of your promise about those sonnets, which you said were at home in your lodge'.[18] Three more 'sonnets' follow, plus prose protestations from Rosader about the beauty of Rosalynd and the importance of his literary performances in 'fixing' this perfection in his mind. Ganymede is allowed one extended speech in response, a critique of the self-indulgence of this mode of being in love – and, itself, an eloquent verbal display:

> 'I can smile,' quoth Ganymede, 'at the sonnetos, canzones, madrigals, rounds and roundelays, that these pensive patients pour out when their eyes are more full of wantonness, than their hearts of passions. Then, as the fishers put the sweetest bait to the fairest fish, so these Ovidians, holding *Amo* in their tongues, when their thoughts come at haphazard, write that they be wrapt in an endless labyrinth of sorrow, when walking in the large lease of liberty, they only have their humours in their inkpot....' (R. 76)

This speech, of which I have quoted only a third, is emotionally and rhetorically similar to Rosalind's swingeing demolition of the grand icons of romantic love:

> No, faith, die by attorney. The poor world is almost six thousand years old, and in all this time there was not any man died in his own person, videlicit, in a love-cause. Troilus had his brains dashed out with a Grecian club, yet he did what he could to die before, and he is one of the patterns of love. Leander, he would have lived many a fair year though Hero had turned nun, if it had not been for a hot mid summer night; for, good youth, he went but forth to wash him in the Hellespont, and being taken with the cramp, was drowned, and the foolish chroniclers of that age found it was Hero of Sestos. But these

are all lies: men have died from time to time and worms have eaten them, but not for love. (4. 1. 89–103)

In Shakespeare's text, just before this flight of witty eloquence, there is a moment of physical tension when Orlando takes the initiative, 'Rosalind' having signalled that she is 'in a holiday humour and like enough to consent' (4. 1. 65–6). Orlando's answer to the challenge, 'What would you say to me now, and I were your very very Rosalind?' is to shift the action onto the physical plane: 'I would kiss before I spoke'. Stage business – an attempted kiss – is clearly implied here, with Rosalind talking fast (and deliberately coarsely, with her mention of spit?) in order to put him off. This brief moment raises the stakes for the watching audience: the fact that the characters' desires are *embodied* in the actors will not be denied: we expect a kiss, if not now, then – all the more urgently for the delay – later.

Lodge is rarely concerned to imagine bodies enacting his story: the delight that he offers his reading audience is in the mind – particularly via the appeal of classical references to the educated reader – and the mind's ear, in the liberal doses of 'sonnetos' which dot the text. The climax of these is the 'wooing Eclogue', a duet between Rosader and Ganymede, in which Ganymede does play the female role. Whereas Orlando's response to the invitation to 'woo' is to offer to kiss, Rosader abides by the rules of courtly love and obeys his 'lady's' command: 'let me see how thou canst woo: I will represent Rosalynd, and thou shalt be as thou art, Rosader. See in some amorous ecologue, how if Rosalynd were present, how thou couldst court her; and while we sing of love, Aliena shall tune her pipe and play us melody' (R. 79). The reader, that is, is to imagine appropriate music accompanying this climactic literary performance.

The eclogue is a 'pastoral dialogue' (*OED*); each long stanza concludes with a variation on 'O Rosalynd, then be thou pitiful, for Rosalynd is only beautiful'. Lodge varies it after three stanzas with the fourth stanza broken into short segments of dialogue as the wooing heats up. 'Rosalynd' gives in, and a triumphant duet follows, 'Oh, gain more great than kingdoms or a crown!'/'Oh, trust betrayed if Rosader abuse me'. Lodge was no doubt familiar with the popular musical mode of the madrigal-dialogue or *pastourelle*; what this scene irresistibly reminds twentieth-century readers of is full-blown opera (an art-form which was, in fact, just beginning to be established as Lodge and Shakespeare were writing). The analogy of tenor and soprano declaring their love for each other and finally uniting in a rapturous *cabaletta* suggests the formality and potential comedy of this scene in Lodge – a risibleness that Shakespeare avoids in favour of something that creates very much more natural-seeming characters:

> ROSALIND But come, now I will be your Rosalind in a more coming-on disposition; and ask me what you will, I will grant it.
> ORLANDO Then love me, Rosalind.
> ROSALIND Yes, faith, will I, Fridays and Saturdays and all.
> ORLANDO And wilt thou have me?
> ROSALIND Ay, and twenty such.
> ORLANDO What sayest thou?
> ROSALIND Are you not good?
> ORLANDO I hope so.
> ROSALIND Why then, can one desire too much of a good thing?
>
> (4. 1. 106–16)

Both these duetting exchanges – Lodge's high art, Shakespeare's colloquial familiarity – lead to the mock-marriage, a scene in Shakespeare which I want to look at in the context of the play's other 'weddings' (see chapter 6). But it is worth noting here that it is Lodge's Aliena who proposes the 'marriage'; she has no hesitation in playing the role of priest. It is Rosalynd/Ganymede whose embarrassed response is recorded: she 'changed as red as a rose. And so with a smile and a blush, they made up this jesting match, that after proved to a marriage in earnest, Rosader full little thinking he had wooed and won his Rosalynd' (*R*. 83). The conversation between the young women after this crucial event illustrates the difference between the two writers' imaginations. Lodge's Aliena, always a more chatty figure than Shakespeare's, begins to 'prattle' with Ganymede, offering the opinion that 'by all probable conjectures, this match will be a marriage'. Ganymede is sceptical: 'Tush...there goes more words to a bargain than one', and so on; and Aliena concludes the exchange by remarking that she hopes Rosalynd will pay more attention to their sheep, now that she is assured of Rosader's love (*R*. 84). The girls seem very companionable in this chatter, their

48

friendship undisturbed by the remarkable event that has just taken place, a public enactment of Rosalynd's and Rosader's commitment to one another.

Very different is Shakespeare's coda to the mock-marriage and subsequent 'flyting' between Rosalind and Orlando. Celia seems irritated, feeling betrayed? – 'You have simply misused our sex in your love-prate. We must have your doublet and hose plucked over your head, and show the world what the bird hath done to her own nest' (4. 1. 191–94).[19] Despite its proverbial origin, the specific image here of stripping off Rosalind's male gender to show a filthy female nakedness is not pleasant. Rosalind replies with an utterance of equally powerful feeling, though very different emotional reference: 'O coz, coz, coz, my pretty little coz, that thou didst know how many fathom deep I am in love! But it cannot be sounded. My affection hath an unknown bottom, like the Bay of Portugal' (4. 1. 195–8). In response to Celia's tart remark ('Or rather bottomless...') she continues to expatiate on her feelings, concluding, 'I'll tell thee Aliena, I cannot be out of sight of Orlando. I'll go find a shadow and sigh till he come.' Rosalind is fully in thrall to love – though she cannot admit or display this feeling to anyone except her more-than-sister friend. It's an emotionally fraught situation, which leaves Celia on her own: no wonder she ends the scene with the weary, or cynical, remark, 'And I'll sleep'. The two women are seen to separate for the first time in the play.

Two patterns of movement suggest themselves here: either Rosalind exits stage left, towards the sheep-cote to wait for Orlando's return, while Celia settles to sleep on stage during the brief huntsmen's scene (4. 2); or Rosalind exits stage right, into the forest, narrowly missing the hunters' entrance from the forest, which happens after Celia's exit stage left towards the cottage for her nap. Whichever way it is played, it leaves the visual image of a situation which is particularly difficult for Celia, since unlike Rosalind she has no anticipation of further pleasurable friction at the next meeting with Orlando. The option taken in Adrian Noble's 1985 RSC production – to leave Celia onstage during the hunters' song – allowed this scene to be presented as invading Celia's unconscious, a dream of defloration, male violence feared yet desired. Noble's psychoanalytic reading created a heightened feeling of sexual frustration and expectation in Celia which was answered by the unexpected arrival of Oliver in the next scene. Significantly, there is much mention of violence and blood in this scene, and Rosalind faints at the sight of the 'bloody napkin', which can be read not only as a symbol of the absent, wounded Orlando, but also as a metonym of her own hidden femininity. Eventually the flirtatious and largely verbal pleasures of 'friction' have to give way to the physical realities of the body, if the play's story is to move out of the artificial world of pastoral into the real world of the audience.

5

How Like You this Shepherd's Life?

As I argued in chapter 3, the Forest of Arden is not an undifferentiated green space: we are invited to imagine different places off behind the two stage-doors, which are symbolically associated – one with male aristocracy and power, and the other with female and working-class people; one deep in the forest, the other on 'the skirts of the forest' where olives are grown and sheep are tended. It is the native inhabitants of that lower-status space that I want to look at in this chapter; they are 'layered' so as to produce a complex critique of certain habits of the aristocracy. They operate via the common Elizabethan literary convention of the pastoral, a genre to which Lodge's romance *Rosalynd* largely belongs.

In the hands of writers such as Lodge, Sidney, and Spenser, pastoral literature created an idealized landscape of love and art, simple and free of physical care (no Shakespearean 'winter winds' blow there). David Young in his book *The Heart's Forest* takes us beyond these generalizations to an analysis of the binary oppositions on which the genre is based:

> The social antitheses are perhaps the most obvious: urban versus rural, court versus country. They could deal variously with manners (polished versus rustic), with class divisions (aristocrat versus commoner), and with economic differences (rich versus poor).[1]

Other oppositional topics, Young suggests, are the active life versus the contemplative, worldliness versus innocence, nurture and nature, Art and Nature and Art and Fortune. If I add masculine versus feminine, I am not just indicating one of the main developments in critical interest in Shakespeare since the publication of Young's book in 1972; I am also arguing for a structuring principle in the play which underlies the simple extractable 'themes' of pastoral. This has been the main emphasis of chapters 1–4; I turn now to more traditional critical material, though I will be offering a reading of it in terms derived from the materialist positions of new historicism.

'The pastoral characters of the play', wrote the scholar W. W. Greg,

> may be roughly analysed as follows. Celia and Rosalind, the latter disguised as a youth, are courtly characters; Phebe and Silvius represent the polished Arcadians of pastoral tradition; while Audrey and William combine the character of farcical rustics with the inimitable humanity which distinguishes Shakepeare's creations. It is noteworthy that this last pair is the dramatist's own addition to the cast.[2]

There are many more scenes which involve the 'pastoral' characters than there are scenes of Duke Senior and his men in the forest proper. This might suggest that the pastoral characters, added to the three principal (pseudo-pastoral) characters of Rosalind, Orlando, and Celia, offer not only more amusement and variety than the aristocrats, but also more complex and nutritious intellectual food to the curious and largely non-aristocratic audience.

Shakespeare's Corin, like Lodge's Coridon, is an old shepherd (2. 4. 22), immune by reason of his age to the pangs of romantic love that afflict Silvius and Orlando and even Touchstone. His age and experience of the economic and physical realities of the shepherd's life give him a wisdom that not all Touchstone's frantic teasing can disturb. There is no doubt that he comes off better in 3.2's discussion with Touchstone of the court versus country debate. Whereas Touchstone's answer to the question 'And how like you this shepherd's life?' is a set of nonsensical (though high-sounding) antitheses ('In respect that it is solitary, I like it very well; but in respect that it is private, it is a very vile life', etc.), Corin's 'philosophy' is proverbial wisdom, easily understood by an audience:

> No more but that I know the more one sickens the worse at ease he is; and that he that wants money, means and content is without three good friends; that the property of rain is to wet and fire to burn; that good pasture makes fat sheep, and that a great cause of

the night is lack of the sun; that he that hath learned no wit by nature nor art may complain of good breeding or comes of a very dull kindred. (3. 2. 23–30)

He goes on to make the commonsense point that 'Those that are good manners at the court are as ridiculous in the country as the behaviour of the country is most mockable at the court' (3. 2. 44–7), instancing particularly the unhygienic courtly habit of kissing hands. And to Touchstone's most frenetic expostulation 'Wilt thou rest damned? God help thee, shallow man! God make incision in thee, thou art raw!', he replies with simple dignity: 'Sir, I am a true labourer: I earn that I eat, get that I wear, owe no man hate, envy no man's happiness, glad of other men's good, content with my harm; and the greatest of my pride is to see my ewes graze and my lambs suck' (3. 2. 71–75).

There is a subtle difference between this statement of pride in an honourable way of life and Lodge's Coridon's equivalent speech, which is a rhetorical utterance whose tenor is entirely based on literary pastoral convention – complete with unlikely Latin tag:

for a shepherd's life, O mistress, did you but live a while in their content, you would say the court were rather a place of sorrow than of solace. Here, mistress, shall not Fortune thwart you, but in mean misfortunes, as the loss of a few sheep, which, as it breeds no beggary, so it can be no extreme prejudice: the next year we may mend all with a fresh increase. Envy stirs not us, we covet not to climb, our desires mount not above our degrees, nor our thoughts above our fortunes. Care cannot harbour in our cottages, nor do our homely couches know broken slumbers: as we exceed not in diet, so we have enough to satisfy; and, mistress, I have so much Latin, *Satis est quod sufficit.*[3]

The difference lies in Corin's proudly seeing himself as 'a true labourer': it connects him to images of working-class pride and incipient revolt in other Shakespearean plays and in the social reality of Elizabethan England – more tellingly for the original audience, perhaps, than the Robin Hood fantasies of the exiled aristocrats. We remember that at their first meeting, Corin told the disguised Celia and Rosalind,

...I am shepherd to another man
And do not shear the fleeces that I graze:

My master is of churlish disposition
And little recks to find the way to heaven
By doing deeds of hospitality.

(2. 4. 76–80)

Corin's pastoral world is subject to the laws of capitalist economy, and the moral failings that so often accompany it, though he himself fulfils the ancient convention of hospitality with unassuming straightforwardness: 'But what is, come see,/ And in my voice most welcome shall you be'.

If Corin represents a recognizable figure from the reality of agricultural England, Silvius, the young shepherd, is entirely locked into a literary mode of being (as Corin tartly remarks, he 'little cares for buying anything', 2. 4. 88). He is playing the role of the disdained lover in the courtly literary tradition which combined elements of the pastoral with the fashion for Petrarchan sonnet-making. The more psychologically realistic characters Corin, Celia, and Rosalind position themselves as onstage audience for Silvius's and Phebe's performance of these roles – thus giving the real audience permission to recognize and laugh at the absurdities of the fashionable literary construction of love:

CORIN If you will see a pageant truly play'd,
Between the pale complexion of true love
And the red glow of scorn and proud disdain,
Go hence a little and I shall conduct you,
If you will mark it.

(3. 4. 48–52)

But an unexpected and frame-breaking event is Rosalind's determination to intervene in 'their play' (l. 55). Her attempt to bring reality to bear on the relationship of this literary couple has results which are both comic and disturbing. But first, we are treated to a thorough satire of Petrarchan attitudes – in terms which reinscribe the play's earlier demonstration of violence as prevalent in relations which should be based in affection, tolerance, respect. Violence, because it is an essential component of the culture's ideal of a dominant masculinity (as the play has already shown), pervades the language even of courtly love:

SILVIUS Sweet Phebe do not scorn me, do not Phebe.
Say that you love me not, but say not so
In bitterness. The common executioner,
Whose heart th'accustom'd sight of death makes hard,
Falls not the axe upon the humbled neck
But first begs pardon: will you sterner be
Than he that dies and lives by bloody drops?

Enter Rosalind, Celia and Corin [behind].

PHEBE I would not be thy executioner;
I fly thee, for I would not injure thee.
Thou tell'st me there is murder in mine eye:
'Tis pretty, sure, and very probable,
That eyes, that are the frail'st and softest things,
Who shut their coward gates on atomies,
Should be call'd tyrants, butchers, murderers.
Now I do frown on thee with all my heart,
And if mine eyes can wound, now let them kill thee.
Now counterfeit to swoon: why now fall down,
Or if thou canst not, O for shame, for shame,
Lie not, to say mine eyes are murderers.
Now show the wound mine eye hath made in thee.
Scratch thee but with a pin, and there remains
Some scar of it; lean but upon a rush,
The cicatrice and capable impressure
Thy palm some moment keeps; but now mine eyes,
Which I have darted at thee, hurt thee not,
Nor, I am sure, there is no force in eyes
That can do hurt.

(3. 5. 1–27)

I doubt if any other Elizabethan shepherdess ever engaged in such trenchant literary criticism of her lover's conventional (and nonsensical) attitudes. It puts Phebe momentarily on a par with the Rosalind of 4. 1. 101–2: 'But these are all lies: men have died from time to time and worms have eaten them, but not for love'. Only momentarily is she a spokesperson for feminine common-sense, however: for Rosalind-as-Ganymede interrupts, and thus brings onto Phebe and Silvius's stage a more complex embodiment of sex and gender than either of them have learnt to perform. No wonder Phebe is fascinated with the glamour of this youth whose speech is so energetic, whose insults even are so eloquent, whose range of metaphor is fresh and rich compared with the antique clichés of Silvius's plaints. This is in fact Rosalind's longest single speech in the play; unusually for her, it is in blank verse, which gives it an extra rhythmic pulse. As Phebe says in her speech after Ganymede has left the stage, 'he talks well...words do well/When he that speaks them pleases those that hear' (3. 5. 110–12) – even when she hears herself insulted in this manner:

> 'Tis not your inky brows, your black silk hair,
> Your bugle eyeballs, nor your cheek of cream
> That can entame my spirits to your worship.
> You foolish shepherd, wherefore do you follow her,
> Like foggy South puffing with wind and rain?
> You are a thousand times a properer man
> Than she a woman. 'Tis such fools as you
> That makes the world full of ill-favour'd children.
> 'Tis not her glass but you that flatters her;
> And out of you she sees herself more proper
> Than any of her lineaments can show her.
> But, mistress, know yourself. Down on your knees
> And thank heaven, fasting, for a good man's love;
> For I must tell you friendly in your ear,
> Sell when you can, you are not for all markets.

> (3. 5. 46–60)

Rosalind's invocation of the reality principle here – and her embodiment of a paradoxically more 'real' sexual energy than Silvius has yet discovered in himself (paradoxical because, as Rosalind says, 'I am falser than vows made in wine', 3. 5. 72–3) – has a transformative effect on Phebe. She begins to move from being merely a literary character towards the model of psychological realism that Shakespeare invented in just such a role as Rosalind. We can hear this in her exchanges with Silvius when Rosalind and the others have left the stage:

> PHEBE Hah? What say'st thou, Silvius?
> SILVIUS Sweet Phebe pity me.
> PHEBE Why, I am sorry for thee gentle Silvius.
>
> .   .   .   .
>
> Know'st thou the youth that spoke to me erewhile?

> (3. 5. 83–5, 105)

Her long speech, ending Act 3, is full of hesitations and contradictions: it demands to be spoken naturalistically, even though it is in blank verse and veers towards the conventions of the blazon or formal praise of the beloved's physical character-istics. But it self-consciously foregrounds the rhetoric of the blazon ('marking him in parcels'), and thus deconstructs the literary convention in favour of a recognition of the confusions caused by desire:

> It is a pretty youth – not very pretty –
> But sure he's proud, and yet his pride becomes him.
> He'll make a proper man. The best thing in him
> Is his complexion; and faster than his tongue
> Did make offence, his eye did heal it up.
> He is not very tall, yet for his years he's tall.
> His leg is but so so; and yet 'tis well.
> There was a pretty redness in his lip,
> A little riper and more lusty red
> Than that mix'd in his cheek; 'twas just the difference
> Betwixt the constant red and mingled damask.
> There be some women Silvius, had they mark'd him
> In parcels as I did, would have gone near
> To fall in love with him: but for my part,
> I love him not, nor hate him not...
>
> (3. 5. 113–27)

Silvius remains content to play the conventional humble servant of his mistress – 'Loose now and then/A scatter'd smile, and that I'll live upon' (3. 5. 103–4); but Phebe has glimpsed a world of real emotional complexity. However, presumably in order not to complicate the play's emotional tapestry too much, Shakespeare allows her to return to her usual literary *modus operandi* to deal with this new situation: 'I'll write to him a very taunting letter,/And thou shalt bear it, wilt thou Silvius?' (3. 5. 134–5). Of course what the hapless Silvius carries to Rosalind is an address in extravagant couplets (reminiscent of Orlando's poetic effusions) declaring Phebe's love: this in turn gives Silvius a taste of reality: 'Call you this chiding?' (4. 3. 64).

Both Silvius and Phebe eventually escape just enough from their literary stereotypes to be of some interest to us in the play's resolution. This is brought about by their intersection with the play's principal pair of lovers, Rosalind and Orlando. Phebe falls in love with Ganymede, as we have seen; Orlando has begun by performing 'being in love' (like Silvius) in the acceptable pastoral manner, by composing poems (sticking them on trees is his particular variety of 'lover's madness') – even his first speech in 3. 2 is in the form of the second and third quatrains and final couplet of an Elizabethan sonnet. Though he does not correspond, as Rosalind points out, to the physical image of a lover (3. 2. 363–74), Orlando is much more energetic and likeably masculine than this effeminized stereotype. Nevertheless, much of Rosalind/Ganymede's teasing of him is directed towards keeping him away from lapsing into the stereotype, and stimulating him rather to bring into play a fully complex physical and intellectual being who responds to her wit and ambiguous bodily presence. But when in 5. 2. 50 he declares in frustration (and perhaps exhaustion!), 'I can live no longer by thinking', he is only too willing to sing in a Petrarchan chorus led by Silvius, which Rosalind roundly declares is 'like the howling of Irish wolves against the moon' (5. 3. 110–11 – her own contribution to the chorus has been a tart undermining of its premise of universal yearning: 'And so am I for no woman').

The play's final pair of pastoral figures are Audrey and William. In the 'real' world, it is these two who would have made one of the 'couples coming to the ark' in the play's last wedding scene. Audrey is a goat-keeper, no pastoral shepherdess but a working member of the rural economy; William, who only appears in 5. 1, is her beau, of the right age, social status and relative wealth ('Art rich?'– 'Faith sir, so so', 5. 1. 24–5) to set up house with Audrey. But Audrey is seduced by Touchstone's promises of worldly splendour at court. It is clear to Jaques – and thus to the audience – that their marriage is but 'two months victuall'd' (5. 4. 191). The function of this unlikely relationship is primarily to expand the court/country opposition which was set up in Touchstone's dialogue with Corin. This time, Touchstone is allowed to score a few more points, though they are in favour of the literature produced by courtly sophistication – and necessarily, therefore, ambivalent:

> TOUCHSTONE ... Truly, I would the gods had made thee poetical.
> AUDREY I do not know what 'poetical' is: is it honest in deed and word? is it a true thing?
> TOUCHSTONE No, truly; for the truest poetry is the most feigning; and lovers are given to poetry, and what they swear in poetry may be said as lovers they do feign.

58

AUDREY Do you wish then that the gods had made me poetical?
TOUCHSTONE I do, truly; for thou swearest to me thou art honest:
now, if thou wert a poet, I might have some hope thou didst feign.

(3. 3. 12–23)

What is being raised here for the audience's subconscious reflection is theatre's basic questioning of the relation between poetry/fiction and the 'real' world. Audrey presents an image of everyday reality, Touchstone of fantasy: this will be visually obvious in the costume contrasts of the 'foul' goat-girl and the motley-clad court jester. Touchstone's speech emphasizes the dishonesty or 'feigning' of poetry, yet we are aware that this point is being made via an instance of 'feigning' – the dramatic scene, here particularly the unlikely coupling of clown and goat-girl. Further, without Audrey's naïve questioning, the demonstration would be stymied: Audrey's realism provides the 'feed' to Touchstone's fantastic wit. Perhaps what we are seeing in Audrey and Touchstone is an emblem of the symbiotic and fruitful relation between art and life, its temporary and always liminal nature emphasized by its very incongruity. Art (Touchstone) will be wandering off after some new topic to use as a base for his games; life (Audrey) will get on with facing the problems of the real economic and emotional world.[4]

6

Wedding Is
Great Juno's Crown

Comedies usually conclude with a wedding, or at least the announcement of one (or more). Biron in *Love's Labour's Lost* is one of many characters in Shakespeare's comedies who speaks for the author's consciousness of the rules of the genre he is working in:

> Our wooing doth not end like an old play.
> Jack hath not Jill. These ladies' courtesy
> Might well have made our sport a comedy.
>
> (*LLL*, 5. 2. 860–62)

Love's Labour's Lost, however, ends with weddings postponed, disrupting the audience's easy romantic expectations and recognizing the need for further reflection (and, in the case of the men, growing up) before the 'world-without-end bargain' of marriage is made. *As You Like It* undertakes its defamiliarizing of the wedding conclusion by offering the audience three variations on the ceremony, placed at strategic moments during the play. It's as if to say, we cannot avoid the imperatives of genre – this is a romantic comedy and we all know that Rosalind and Orlando will end up blissfully together – but what is the relation between the euphoric ritual of the wedding and the realities of the social world to which a marriage ties two lovers? In *Shakespeare's Comic Rites* Edward Berry argues that

> if Shakespeare lived in a ritualistic culture, in which ceremony gave conscious shape even to the reflexes of daily life, he also lived in a culture in which the role of ritual was becoming increasingly problematic, even to the point of fragmenting the very community it should have sustained.[1]

The issue was part of the wider debate between Puritans and traditional Anglicans which was ultimately to result in civil war in the early part of the seventeenth century. Puritans disapproved of ceremony, associating it not only with the potential for rioting and drunkenness (like theatre), but also with the practices of the Catholic church, from which England had been painfully weaning itself throughout the sixteenth century. The belief that a priest was the only authoritative expounder of the word of God, and the quasi-magical notion that the Christian's spiritual life could be regulated through the seven sacraments: such ideas were examined, critiqued, and reinscribed in a very limited way as the Anglican church became the 'reformed' Church of England, with the monarch as its head. But the debates continued as the Puritan wing of the church sought ever greater reform in the direction of a private and personal conduct of the spiritual life. At the end of the century, *As You Like It*, ending triumphantly in a wedding feast which deliberately eschews Christian reference, enters obliquely but disconcertingly into these debates, taking advantage once again of theatre's position in 'the liberties' of civic society.

The first attempted wedding we see in the play is that between Touchstone and Audrey in 3. 3. Touchstone, determined to have the sexual pleasure that is offered by the association of Audrey with goats (which were traditional images of lasciviousness – though Audrey insists that she is 'honest', i.e. chaste), has tried to arrange a cheap and quick marriage, on the grounds, as he later tells us, that it 'were better to be married of [Sir Oliver] than of another: for he is not like to marry me well; and not being well married, it will be a good excuse for me hereafter to leave my wife' (3. 3. 81–5). The minister whom he has engaged is Sir Oliver Martext, 'the vicar of the next village' (3. 3. 37), who is obviously willing to come out to do the business rather than have it conducted more solemnly in the parish church. This clergyman would have been a character very recognizable to the original audience as an embodiment of stereotyped rustic ignorance, a view which had a historical basis at this time. Sir Oliver is an exemplar of Warwickshire's 'many incompetent clergymen, "dumbe and vnlearned," a notorious and well documented group'.[2] The historian Ronald Bayne contextualizes this phenomenon:

['Sir'] came to be applied especially to the old-fashioned or ignorant priest who could only read the services and was not able to preach. The reforming party were unwilling that such readers should be recognized as clergy, and the more extreme among them insisted on the necessity of the 'ministry of the word' or preaching, to constitute a valid ministry.... The changes at Edward's accession, at Mary's accession, and at Elizabeth's accession, tended generally to eliminate the best parish priests, and to lower the standard both of piety and learning among those that were left....The poor pay of the parish priest was a main cause of his illiteracy and inefficiency.[3]

Sir Oliver is thus part of the play's ongoing argument about the value of that complex signifier of civilization, literature/literacy. He knows the basic ecclesiastical laws – 'Truly she must be given, or the marriage is not lawful' (3. 3. 63) – but cannot, as Jaques points out, 'tell you what marriage is', cannot provide the spiritual counsel arising from study that may equip Touchstone and Audrey for the difficulties of this ill-matched marriage (interestingly, Jaques offers to 'counsel' them instead, 3. 3. 86). So this version of the argument would seem to be won by the court or city position, represented by the philosopher Jaques. Sir Oliver is a figure of comic inefficiency, an easy butt for the sophisticated wits (here a fearsome duo) of Jaques and Touchstone, affording amusement to the city audience. But he does have the last word in the scene, and it's oddly subversive of their authority and his so-called incompetence: ' 'Tis no matter. Ne'er a fantastical knave of them all shall flout me out of my calling' (3. 3. 97–8). He suffers no loss of *amour-propre*, he knows he has a calling, a profession (like Corin); however humble it be, it is more honourable than to be merely a 'fantastical knave', which the duo of wits too often are (see chapter 7's discussion of the symbiosis of Jaques and Touchstone). His exit back to his village (stage left) has the resonance of a return to social reality; Touchstone and Audrey go further, deeper (stage right), into the centre of the forest with Jaques, where the utopian community of Duke Senior is living out its fantasies.

Thus, a marriage between Audrey and Touchstone is postponed until it can be performed with the proper ceremony, as we expect it will be at the end of the play. But the text's next approach to the ceremony plays with and overrides, in a completely unexpected way, notions of ecclesiastical propriety and authority. It occurs as the climax of 4. 1, the long wooing scene between Orlando and Ganymede/Rosalind, of which Celia is the onstage audience. 'Rosalind' is very much in authority as this sequence begins; she has just eloquently deconstructed the romance convention of the male lover dying for love, and now expertly inverts the stereotype of passive and distant beloved: 'But come, now I will be your Rosalind in a more coming-on disposition; and ask me what you will, I will grant it' (4. 1. 106–7), an exchange concluding with her triumphant, 'Why then, can one desire too much of a good thing?'

Rosalind's combination of robust commonsense and lightning wit sets up the conditions for the direction in which she next takes the scene: 'Come sister, you shall be the priest and marry us'. Anything seems possible by this stage in this exhilarating courtship of girl (or boy, disguised as boy pretending to be girl) – and boy. But for the other girl to (pretend to) 'be the priest'? to take on, in a highly ambiguous 'play' situation, the role of patriarchal religious authority? No wonder Celia's immediate response is 'I cannot say the words'. She turns the ambiguity of the situation momentarily to her own defence: does this mean 'I will not transgress gender and ecclesiastical decorum' or 'I am unable to remember the words'?[4] Undaunted, Rosalind supplies the very words of the Anglican marriage service: 'You must begin, "Will you Orlando –"' and thereby prompts her cousin to perform a wedding ceremony that would have seemed quite legal to the Elizabethan audience. Agnes Latham discusses the legal validity of what is shown on stage here: 'Canon law accepted that any kind of marriage was better than no marriage.... Marriage *per verba de praesenti* [declared as of now] was still valid in the sixteenth century. The church disapproved, unless its blessing was subsequently asked', but failure to do this did not invalidate the marriage. Latham points out that Rosalind's interruptions in the 'service' show that she 'knows precisely what she is doing...she rejects the grammatically ambiguous "I will" and insists upon the vital present tense.... "you must say, 'I take thee Rosalind for wife'."'[5]

The audience, thus, hears the words of a valid marriage ceremony. What they see, however, is a very different phenomenon from the images that normally would be part of the ceremony. They see a female priest, and they see the 'bride' apparently a male (even though Ganymede pretends to be Rosalind 'he' remains dressed as a boy).

The prohibition against women priests goes back a long way in the history of the Christian church. St Paul's first epistle to Timothy, 2:12, asserts, 'But I suffer not a woman to teach, nor to usurp authority over the man, but to be in silence'. This directive chimed well with the patriarchal order of Elizabethan England, despite the paradoxical example of the Queen, educated intellectual, astute politician, head of the Church of England by virtue of her father's rejection of the authority of Rome. She was the exception that proved the rule. Nevertheless, under the impetus of the Reformation, some sects did accept women as pastors and prophets – the Anabaptists, for example. For Celia to be identified momentarily with one of these figures – sacrilegious Anglican *or* member of a utopianist sect – is further to reinforce the carnivalesque and liminal nature of the theatrical experience. Whatever way the audience looks at it, the mock-marriage both instantiates the law and defies patriarchal order.

Then there is the question of whether what the audience is watching is a same-sex marriage. The original audience saw an adult male 'marrying' a boy – at the same time as they saw the more innocuous representation of a girl (in the theatrical conventions of the time) marrying a man. Except that the girl is wearing boy's clothes; so that the transgressive nature of what is being enacted is even more visually present (even to a modern audience, where a female actor plays the role). Valerie Traub, in the course of her examination of the circulating homoerotics of Shakespearean comedy, argues that this moment

> legitimizes the multiple desires it represents. The point is not that Orlando and Ganymede formalize a homosexual marriage, but rather that as the distance between Rosalind and Ganymede collapses, distinctions between homoerotic and heterosexual collapse as well. As the woman and the shepherd boy merge, Orlando's words resound with the conviction that, for the moment, he (as much as Rosalind and the audience) is engaged in the ceremony as if it were real.[6]

Traub's explanation comes close, I think, to describing the effect of this extraordinary moment: in short, Shakespeare has scripted a scene (subtly reworking the hints offered by Lodge) that allows everyone in the audience an experience of romantic bliss – whether their sexual tastes are homosexual, heterosexual, or both. It subverts, as Traub concludes, the 'reduction [in heterosexual matrimony] of the plurality of desire into the singularity of monogamy'.

One final reason for Celia's reluctance to 'say the words' is to do with this play's peculiar self-awareness. To speak, as she does, the words of the Prayer Book on a public stage was a punishable offence even before James I's Act against stage profanity:

> the Act of Uniformity at the beginning of Elizabeth's reign provided severe penalties 'if any Person or Persons whatsoever... shall in any Enterludes, Plays, Songs, Rhimes, or by other open Words declare or speak any thing in the derogation, depraving, or despising of the same Book, or of any thing therein contained....' This made it impossible to use portions of the services of the church, or anything approximating them, in a play; and the marriage ceremony... could not be suggested.[7]

Or rather, it could not be completed, as it is here in essence (there is an interrupted marriage ceremony, complete with priest, in *Much Ado About Nothing*). Rosalind's burst of witty verbosity after the crucial words 'I do take thee Orlando for my husband' have been spoken arises from the same sense of relief as the coarse jokes that occur at wedding breakfasts – jokes that dispel a lingering dismay at the commitment to the long road ahead through an invocation of an almost uncontrollable sexual energy:

> ROSALIND ... No, no, Orlando, men are April when they woo, December when they wed. Maids are May when they are maids, but the sky changes when they are wives. I will be more jealous of thee than a Barbary cock-pigeon over his hen, more clamorous than a parrot against rain, more new-fangled than an ape, more giddy in my desires than a monkey. I will weep for nothing, like Diana in the fountain, and I will do that when you are disposed to be merry. I will laugh like a hyen, and that when thou art inclined to sleep.
>
> ORLANDO But will my Rosalind do so?
>
> ROSALIND By my life, she will do as I do.
>
> ORLANDO O but she is wise.
>
> ROSALIND Or else she could not have the wit to do this: the wiser, the waywarder. Make the doors upon a woman's wit, and it will out at the casement; shut that and 'twill out at the key-hole; stop that, 'twill fly with the smoke out at the chimney.
>
> (4. 1. 138–56)

As the repartee and the parody of marital quarrelling continues, the audience is convinced that whatever else this marriage may be, it will never be dull. And that judgement is underlined by Rosalind's declaration 'in her own person' after Orlando has left the stage to 'attend the Duke at dinner' (as in, 'I'm off to the pub with me mates now'), 'O coz, coz, coz, my pretty little coz, that thou didst know how many fathom deep I am in love! But it cannot be sounded: my affection hath an unknown bottom, like the bay of Portugal' (4. 1. 195–8).

Whatever has been the complex game played in the mock-wedding – and it is, as we have seen, a strikingly transgressive moment however one reads it – in this speech and the following one, it is clear that Rosalind is head over heels in love. The problem then is how to move, within the main frame of theatrical pretence, to a representation of a 'more true' wedding, one in which there is no longer any need for pretence, and game-playing is replaced by a ceremony which is recognized by the whole community as valorizing romantic love. The play does this by a remarkable double *coup de théâtre*, in the last scene and the Epilogue, a progression of events which celebrates Rosalind's power, takes it away from her, and then returns it to her.

The winding-up of the play's love stories begins in 5. 2, with its delightfully arbitrary plot-development:

> ORLANDO Is't possible, that on so little acquaintance you should like her? That but seeing, you should love her? And loving woo? And wooing, she should grant? And will you persever to enjoy her?
> OLIVER Neither call the giddiness of it in question, the poverty of her, the small acquaintance, my sudden wooing, nor her sudden consenting. But say with me, I love Aliena; say with her that she loves me; consent with both, that we may enjoy each other.
>
> (5. 2. 1–9)

Orlando's consent is of course given, and he initiates the plans for a wedding – 'tomorrow. Thither will I invite the Duke and all's contented followers.' But the arrival of his 'Rosalind' ensures that his apparent control of matters is illusory, that 'There is more in it', as Celia has just reminded us in the previous scene of Rosalind's fainting (4. 3. 159).

Orlando voices his discontent to Ganymede, 'I can live no longer by thinking' (5. 2. 50): when his brother is about to enter into the real-life, embodied state of matrimony, mind-games based on the literature of courtly love cannot satisfy. In response to this crisis in their once-playful relationship, Rosalind makes the extraordinary claim that she can solve it all by magic. She offers Orlando a second wedding ceremony, this time with the real Rosalind, 'human as she is' – 'if' (the word is repeated several times) this is what he really wants. It is in a sense Rosalind's final testing of Orlando: can he accept the move into the real world, full adulthood, if that too is engineered by this charismatic shepherd boy rather than by the parental figure offstage right, Duke Senior? The arrival of Silvius and Phebe, with their unthinking acceptance of literary attitudes to love, gives Orlando a little breathing space to contemplate this proposition. This could be a very tense moment, played against the apparent comic intentions of the text: it is to Orlando's credit that he both accepts the impossibility of the situation – he speaks 'To her that is not here, nor doth not hear' – and embraces the possibility of its solution. He will not fail to be at the wedding ceremony, one not organized by the Duke but according to the 'commands' of Ganymede, who 'can do strange things' (5. 2. 59–60). If Celia is a reluctant temporary priest, Rosalind/Ganymede is a magus positively revelling in her powers: the repeated 'I will's of her last speech in this scene resonate with authority.

Much of this authority is put into question by the play's last scene, at the same time as it is paradoxically reasserted by Rosalind's control of the theatrical moment. At the beginning of the scene she (still as Ganymede) ritually hands over the proceedings to the Duke: 'You say, if I bring in your Rosalind,/ You will bestow her on Orlando here?' But then she takes control again, as she checks on the commitment of Silvius, Phebe, and Orlando, concluding,

> I have promis'd to make all this matter even.
> Keep you your word, O Duke, to give your daughter,
> You yours, Orlando, to receive his daughter;
> Keep your word Phebe, that you'll marry me,
> Or else refusing me, to wed this shepherd.
> Keep your word Silvius, that you'll marry her
> If she refuse me: and from hence I go,
> To make these doubts all even.
>
> (5. 4. 18–25)

In fact, as the audience anticipates, she goes to resume her proper dress as a woman. When she returns with Celia, they are accompanied by Hymen, the Greek god of marriage. The role is usually doubled with one of the lesser characters in the play: in my experience, William, Corin, Amiens, even Sir Oliver Martext, though whether their original identities shine through to make some sort of comment on the new role varies. This brings us to the question of the significance of Hymen and his (or her, as in the RSC's 1996 production, which produced a modern marriage-celebrant from the audience) priest-like role. His speech, a rhyming poem in varied metre, begins solemnly:

> Then is there mirth in heaven,
> When earthly things made even
>   Atone together.
> Good Duke receive thy daughter,
> Hymen from heaven brought her,
>   Yea brought her hither,
> That thou mightst join her hand with his
> Whose heart within his bosom is.

(5. 4. 107–14)

The mention of heaven and atonement has recognizably Christian overtones, yet there is no suggestion of a Christian marriage ceremony here as there was in the play's two earlier 'wedding' scenes. Instead a new ritual is spoken and enacted:

> Peace, ho! I bar confusion:
> 'Tis I must make conclusion
>   Of these most strange events.
> Here's eight that must take hands
> To join in Hymen's bands,
>   If truth holds true contents.
> You and you no cross shall part.
> You and you are heart in heart.
> You to his love must accord,
> Or have a woman to your lord.
> You and you are sure together,
> As the winter to foul weather.

(5. 4. 124–135)

Two interpretative possibilities present themselves: Hymen must be seen to be either a rustic performer in a masque produced by Rosalind (which could serve as an interesting recuperation of the discredited court literature), in which case she has dictated the speech to him; or he/she, within the world of the play is 'real', a *deus ex machina* magically conjured by Rosalind, who brings the blessings and power of a pagan world to the story's end. Hymen thus is 'produced' by Rosalind's magical authority, here running closely parallel to that of the writer, and embodying the power of theatre, a power that surprises even the philosophical Duke with the 'truth in sight' that it offers. Further, the song that Hymen commands is certainly no patriarchal Christian hymn; it is paganistic – 'Hymen peoples every town' – and celebrates matriarchal power within the domestic establishment:

> Wedding is great Juno's crown,
> O blessed bond of board and bed.
> 'Tis Hymen peoples every town;
> High wedlock then be honoured.
> Honour, high honour and renown
> To Hymen, god of every town!

(5. 4. 140–45)

Hymen is a curiously slippery figure, who despite his or her appearance as a god can destabilize the play's apparent move towards closure (and there are two more unexpected events – the arrival of Jaques de Boys and Rosalind's Epilogue – to further undermine complacency). The presentation of this figure is a crucial decision to be made by the director and actors of the play, because on it hinges the sort of assent we give to the final marriages. The British actresses Juliet Stevenson and Fiona Shaw, in a joint essay about the unconventional 1985–6 RSC production by Adrian Noble, describe the problem of the ending as they perceived it – and the varying solutions and compromises that were applied to the problem:

> Rosalind, ever-changing, becomes a sort of ring-mistress, drawing together all the threads in the play; a kind of conjuror, creating a collective ritual out of the chaos, and rewarding faith with mysterious revelation. She is now both man and woman, in a way, and as such can transcend reality to become a creature of magic who brings a god to her wedding. But if the play has moved onto another plane now, the last act remains problematical for actresses... it is Duke Senior who resumes charge, and traditional values seem in danger of being celebrated. This, at the end of a play which so fully

and radically explores the complexities of sexuality, maleness, and femaleness, and sends gender boundaries flying, was endlessly difficult to play....

In Stratford Hymen had been represented as a flickering silhouette on a lighted screen, placed upstage, obliging the actors to turn away from the audience to perceive him – this both threw the focus onto an unlikely manifestation which threatened the audience's capacity to believe in what was going on, and deprived them of the characters' responses to the deity and his dictates. In London, Hymen became a mere beam of light whose source was *behind* the audience, so that the actors beheld him facing out front. In this way, the audience was able to focus not on the god, but on the faces of those whose futures he is deciding. This afforded each of us the opportunity to play against the 'happy ever after' element, if we chose.[8]

The performance of Hymen, that is, can either reinforce or subvert the incorporation of Rosalind and Celia back into the patriarchal order represented by the father/uncle Duke Senior. It is true, and disconcerting to modern audiences, that Rosalind's last words in the play are gracefully submissive to that order:

[*To Duke Senior*] To you I give myself, for I am yours.
[*To Orlando*] To you I give myself, for I am yours.

   .   .   .   .   .   .

I'll have no father, if you be not he.
I'll have no husband, if you be not he.
[*To Phebe*] Nor ne'er wed woman, if you be not she.

(5. 4. 115–16, 121–3)

But it is also true that Rosalind is given a last word, after the wedding celebration, after the dance and its interruption by Jaques de Boys with his tale of reconciled brothers. She reclaims verbal authority despite its not being 'the fashion [i.e. acceptable behaviour] to see the lady the epilogue'; she breaks the frame of the play and, as Valerie Traub observes, 'address[es] the audience in a distinctly erotic manner':

'If I were a woman I would kiss as many of you as had beards that pleas'd me, complexions that lik'd me, and breaths that I defied not.' ... the effect of this statement is to highlight the constructed-ness of gender and the flexibility of erotic attraction at precisely the point when the formal impulse of comedy would be to essentialize and fix both gender and eroticism.[9]

Rosalind, boy or girl, shepherd or bride, in her unexpected last appearance reasserts her role as the ultimate witty wordsmith, a role which allows her the freedom that is otherwise only available to the theatre's clowns (in *Twelfth Night* Feste the clown sings the epilogue which takes the audience back to their everyday lives). It is to this play's contrasted pair of clown/commentators, Jaques and Touchstone, that we now turn.

7

All the World's a Stage

When Jaques launches into the play's most famous speech in 2. 5, he is performing several important functions. At the simplest dramaturgic level, as we realize at the speech's conclusion, his disquisition on the seven ages of man creates the impression of time passing, a cover for Orlando's absence from the stage as he goes to rescue old Adam. He enters, supporting or even carrying Adam, just as Jaques speaks the lines that Adam's presence exemplifies:

> Last scene of all,
> That ends this strange eventful history,
> Is second childishness and mere oblivion,
> Sans teeth, sans eyes, sans taste, sans everything.
>
> (2. 7. 163–6)

At the most obvious level of signification, Jaques' speech is a moralization or secular sermon, complete with illustration. But its very rhetoric, its carefully elaborated use of the Elizabethan commonplace *Totus mundus agit histrionem*, points also to its self-consciousness, to a recognition that the speaker is an actor on a stage, with a dual audience – the Duke and his retainers in the play's story, and the watchers of the scene in the Globe theatre. Much of the pleasure to be had from this play and other Shakespearean comedies arises from the acknowledgement of this stage–audience collaboration, a sophisticated playing with the very idea of theatre. The audience, as Michael Mangan argues, enjoys a dual consciousness:

> One convention of the stage demands that an audience 'believe' in the reality of that which is being represented; another simultaneous convention stresses the importance of remembering that what is happening is indeed a performance. In Shakespeare's comedies

these two apparently opposing conventions are repeatedly played off against each other, and the resulting incongruity is exploited. Incongruity is one of the great sources of laughter.[1]

As well as laughter, there is also the pleasure to be gained from watching a virtuoso perform, whether it be juggling with clubs or playing with words, as Jaques is doing here. Because of Shakespeare's linguistic genius, almost all the characters in a Shakespearean comedy have the opportunity to display this virtuosity; but most specifically, it is the province of the stage's clowns. Their job, both within the play's fictional community and within the conventions of the Elizabethan theatre, is solely to entertain and comment on the action. They play little or no part in the plot development; consequently, they tend to be 'wanderers' on the stage, unpredictable in their appearances and (in terms of the symbolic significance of offstage space) not clearly associated with one door or the other, relatively careless of the hierarchy of power.

As Edward Berry argues, the clown is a liminal figure, existing on the margins of the narrative:

> What touches our imagination most directly is not [the clown's] dramatic function, thematic or otherwise . . . but some mysterious energy that is released by the role itself and by its characteristic rhythms of speech and action. This is a peculiarly liminal energy...[2]

This seems likely to be an accurate description of the unique presence and effect of the clown in Elizabethan drama. As Berry concludes, he is 'a figure for the confusion of the liminal stage'.[3] A striking embodiment of this was in Terry Hands's *Twelfth Night* for the RSC in 1979: Feste was always on stage – if not in a scene, sitting at its edge, sometimes watching, sometimes with his back turned. *As You Like It* has two figures on the margins of the action, two observers and commentators: Jaques, the satirist of the court in exile, and Touchstone, the play's official clown.

Touchstone is referred to in the stage directions of the First Folio simply as 'Clowne', that is, the role written for the acting company's clown, in this case probably Robert Armin.[4] The character typically plays on his audience's awareness of his specific theatrical role when he says, of Audrey's country wooer, 'It is meat and drink to me to see a clown. By my troth, we that have good wits have much to answer for: we shall be flouting:

we cannot hold', in 5. 1. 10–12; he also addresses Corin in 2. 4. 62 with 'Holla, you clown!' Touchstone is deliberately using the older connotation of 'clown' as 'rustic fellow' in order to suggest that as a court jester he is superior to them intellectually, but as we have seen this is not the case: Corin and William simply have different priorities, based on the fact that they earn respectable livings working on the land.

The play's other clown, if we go by dramatic function, is undoubtedly Jaques, who himself seems to be aware of this likeness. He is fascinated and delighted by Touchstone, as though he sees in him his own self in a fairground distorting mirror. In retrospect, this is accurate: not only do the two characters share a cynicism towards the other members of the forest communities and a habit of critical repartee in scenes with them, but Touchstone has already performed for Jaques' own benefit in 2. 7. 26–8 a version of the 'seven ages of man' speech ('And so from hour to hour, we ripe, and ripe,/And then from hour to hour, we rot, and rot, and thereby hangs a tale'). The fact that Jaques is able to recite it suggests that he will be inspired to produce his own version at the appropriate moment to come, later in this scene. Indeed his raptures on finding Touchstone in the forest seem to encourage him to develop his own role in the exiled Duke's court beyond that of the sentimental moralizer and professional melancholic whom we heard about in 2. 1. He was only able to indulge his invective against 'The body of country, city, court' in private at that point. Now a whole new possible profession opens before him:

> JAQUES A fool, a fool ! I met a fool i' th' forest,
> A motley fool: a miserable world!
>
> .   .   .   .   .   .
>
> O worthy fool! One that hath been a courtier,
> And says, if ladies be but young and fair,
> They have the gift to know it. And in his brain,
> Which is as dry as the remainder biscuit
> After a voyage, he hath strange places cramm'd
> With observation, the which he vents
> In mangled forms. O that I were a fool!
> I am ambitious for a motley coat.
> DUKE SENIOR Thou shalt have one.
> JAQUES It is my only suit...

(2. 7. 12–13, 36–43)

The word-play and longing for motley (the court fool's garment) as a sign of his professional role and identity is significant. Jaques goes on to claim that he wants the 'liberty/ Withal, as large a charter as the wind,/To blow on whom I please, for so fools have' (2. 7. 47–9). He seems here to indicate a consciousness of that licence which is peculiar to the theatre (in its suburban 'liberties') and to a type of theatrical role which as a courtier and a gentleman he would not be permitted:

> Invest me in my motley. Give me leave
> To speak my mind, and I will through and through
> Cleanse the foul body of th'infected world,
> If they will patiently receive my medicine.
>
> (2. 7. 58–61)

Jaques wants to be accepted as the type of professional social commentator known as the satirist, a literary mode which was particularly fashionable in the late sixteenth century.

> As a literary genre it has a natural affinity with pastoral, both genres being essentially unsympathetic to, or critical of, contemporary urban life.... Books and pamphlets of social satire, both in verse and in prose, sold and circulated widely in the London of the 1590s. The satirists launched attacks on a range of social abuses (such as drunkenness, flattery, ambition and so on) and on various social groups and professions (such as lawyers, courtiers, churchmen).[5]

Mangan points out that many such pamphlets had titles which prefigure Jaques' description of his function, medicinal and purgative. Shakespeare allows the more earthy clown Touchstone (who follows his desires rather than being disgusted by them) to underline the significance of Jaques' name, a pun on 'jakes', a privy or latrine: 'Good even, good Master What-ye-call't' (3. 3. 66) – that is, Master Unmentionable. The satirist's role is that of a processor of human filth, a necessary article. It takes one to know one, as the Duke points out: Jaques has been a 'libertine', has previously allowed himself the liberty to add to the 'embossed sores and headed evils' of the world in his travels (which he describes to Rosalind in 4. 1). The freedom that a professional fool (or actor) has is 'licensed', that is, it has a positive place in society despite its apparent disrespect for authority. By contrast, the freedom or excessive 'licence' which a gentleman indulges in in disregard of his responsibilities eventually leads to the diseased state of society which Jaques now wants to correct through satire. At the end of the play, he will retreat even further from that younger travelling or wandering self which now so disgusts him, causing his melancholy (4. 1. 10–19): in conversation with the converted Duke Frederick, he says, 'There is much matter to be heard and learn'd' (5. 4. 184). His parting remarks, a kind of blessing on the four couples to be married, suggest that, despite his cynical satirist's demeanour, he is willing to see some good in the re-ordered society of the play's end, though it is not for him: 'So to your pleasures. I am for other than for dancing measures' (5. 4. 191–2).

In proper clown/commentator fashion, Jaques has only a minimal role in the plot: interestingly, his only material interference is in stopping the too-casual marriage of Touchstone and Audrey – perhaps he recognizes the impulses of his younger self and wants to save his alter ego Touchstone, at least momentarily, from them? Yet it is arguable that as he travels out of the closed world of the play's end, he can be seen to be continuing a different journey of his own. According to our critical tastes, we may read this as the spiritual development of an interesting character in the play (as the actor playing the role almost inevitably will), or as a sign that the play's euphoric image of completion, reincorporation into the social world, is not an absolute and inevitable end – it is relevant to the needs of the majority only. In this way I would want to refigure Berry's important observation, as regards the dual clowns of *As You Like It*:

> while the dynamics of the plays are progressive and integrative, moving through liminality to incorporation, the clown remains fixed in confusion, sometimes outside and alone. When he plays an important part at the end of a comedy, the clown usually reminds us of human recalcitrance.[6]

Jaques, as clown-like wanderer and commentator, remains a figure of dissent at the end of the play; Touchstone, at least temporarily, is incorporated into a renewed patriarchal society headed by the hopeful, young, and loving couple Orlando and Rosalind.

Touchstone is Jaques' grotesque double, the professional clown.[7] His name, significantly, is only given in the forest scenes – it is an *alias*, chosen by himself, presumably, as Celia's and Rosalind's were. It connotes that which 'serves to test or try the genuineness of anything' (*OED*) – a self-image which aligns him with the satirist Jaques. In fact he never lives up to this self-image: his impulse to perform the more traditional role of the clown is far stronger. As Jensen says, 'he is always "on."' As a character in the play, his performative behavior often seems irrelevant both to the comedy's design and to the comic life around him'; he is 'a stand-up comedian'.[8] There is no doubt about this: his opening performance on the pancakes and the mustard and his closing show-stopper (and time-filler – Rosalind has to change back into her woman's dress) on the degrees of the lie are classic pieces, received as such by their onstage audience. But I cannot agree completely with Jensen that he is 'a figure never wholly integrated into the play's overall movement',[9] despite his bravura performances. Unlike Feste of *Twelfth Night*, who exists as a wanderer *between* the two sources of power (Orsino's and Olivia's houses), Touchstone aligns himself strikingly with the exiled young women – Celia says 'He'll go along o'er the wide world with me'(1. 3. 128), and he does, despite loud complainings about the greater comfort to be found 'at home' in Duke Frederick's service.

Further, there is the curious business of Touchstone's marriage. He is the only one of Shakespeare's fools to marry in the course of the play: he is included, in however qualified a way, in the final mass wedding celebrations ('you to your wrangling, for thy loving voyage/Is but for two months victuall'd' says Jaques, 5. 4. 190–91). This is an event which is deliberately led up to throughout the second half of the play; it does not come out of the blue in the way that, for example, Sir Toby's marriage to Maria is announced in *Twelfth Night*.

Following his ritual fulfilment of his jester's role in the court versus country argument with Corin in 3. 1, Touchstone's next appearance is as the satirist of Orlando's courtly love verses:

> *If a hart do lack a hind,*
> *Let him seek out Rosalind.*
> *If the cat will after kind,*
> *So be sure will Rosalind.*
> *Winter'd garments must be lin'd,*
> *So must slender Rosalind.*
> *They that reap must sheaf and bind,*

> *Then to cart with Rosalind.*
> *Sweetest nut hath sourest rind,*
> *Such a nut is Rosalind.*
> *He that sweetest rose will find,*
> *Must find love's prick, and Rosalind.*

(3. 2. 99–110)

His satire takes the form of a set of sexual innuendoes which expose the physical desire underlying the lover's high-flown verses. With this performance, Touchstone presents himself unequivocally as the play's sign of the *body* and its needs (in fact this was signalled in his first utterance on arriving in Arden, 'I care not for my spirits, if my legs were not weary', 2. 4. 2). His courtship and marriage of Audrey is a necessary counterpoint to the witty intellectual courtship of Rosalind/Ganymede and Orlando and the extravagantly literary relationship of Silvius and Phebe. This emphasis is made very clear in the interrupted wedding scene of 3. 3:

> TOUCHSTONE Come apace good Audrey. I will fetch up your goats, Audrey. And how, Audrey, am I the man yet? Doth my simple feature content you?
> AUDREY Your features? Lord warrant us! What features!
> TOUCHSTONE I am here with thee and thy goats, as the most capricious poet, honest Ovid, was among the Goths.

(3. 3. 1–6)

Goats and Ovid are both associated with lustfulness. Touchstone goes on to speculate on Audrey's 'foulness' and potential 'sluttishness' – i.e. her sexual vigour (in appropriately grotesque carnivalesque terms), but concludes by agreeing with Jaques that he will be married properly: 'Come sweet Audrey,/We must be married or we must live in bawdry' (3. 3. 87–8). He is more than willing, that is, to accept the ideology of patriarchal domesticity, despite his rueful recognition of the danger of cuckoldry: 'As a walled town is more worthier than a village, so is the forehead of a married man more honourable than the bare brow of a bachelor' (3. 3. 52–5).

The unexpected theme of the importance of marriage to Touchstone continues in his next scene (5. 1), in which he overbearingly insists to William that 'I am he...that must marry this woman' (5. 1. 43–5). Scene 3 of this act begins with

78

Touchstone saying, 'Tomorrow is the joyful day, Audrey. Tomorrow will we be married', which is a lead-in to the song 'It was a lover and his lass' – a musical celebration of the *carpe diem* motif which insists that sexual pleasure must be taken when time and bodies are ripe for it. The song prepares the mood and passes the time until the wedding day begins with the next scene: a scene in which Touchstone announces himself and Audrey as 'press[ing] in ... amongst the rest of the country copulatives' (5. 4. 55), despite the unexpectedness of marriage between what Jaques calls 'a pair of very strange beasts, which in all tongues are called fools' (5. 4. 36–8). Touchstone's aside 'Bear your body more seeming, Audrey' (5. 4. 67) suggests a sense of decorum that is foreign to the grotesque carnivalesque body: his wedding is a sign of his (temporary) progression beyond the usually immutable state of clown. It includes him in the play's major narrative and its closure although, like Jaques, he makes no contribution to the plot after Act 1. For two months, at least, Touchstone will lead the life of a married man and responsible member of the community, though like Jaques we might well wonder whether he will be able to curb his tongue from 'wrangling'. For Touchstone's final performance in the play is the virtuosic 'degrees of the lie' speech, a display of his professional abilities as a court jester and theatrical clown, not, one feels, a respectable goat-keeper.

MUCH VIRTUE IN *IF*

'Your If is the only peacemaker: much virtue in If' is the famous tag with which Touchstone winds up the 'degrees of the lie' performance. It is an unexpected conclusion, a rhetorical flourish which in retrospect seems entirely appropriate. There *is* much virtue in If; theatre is based on this assumption, and this play in particular is riddled with Ifs. Here (with my emphases throughout) is a sample of those Ifs which provide the plot's basic progressions, and some of those which signal the play's awareness of its own hypothetical quality:

> CELIA Herein I see thou lovest me not with the full weight that I love thee. *If* my uncle, thy banished father, had banished thy uncle, the Duke my father, so thou hadst been still with me, I could have

taught my love to take thy father for mine: so wouldst thou, *if* the
truth of thy love to me were so righteously tempered as mine is to
thee.

(1. 2. 7–13)

ORLANDO *If* ever you have look'd on better days,
  If ever been where bells have knoll'd to church,
  If ever sat at any good man's feast,
  If ever from your eyelids wiped a tear
  And know what 'tis to pity and be pitied...

(2. 7. 113–17)

TOUCHSTONE Why, *if* thou never wast at court, thou never sawest
good manners; *if* thou never sawest good manners, then thy
manners must be wicked; and wickedness is sin, and sin is
damnation. Thou art in a parlous state, shepherd.

(3. 2. 39–43)

ROSALIND I would cure you, *if* you would but call me Rosalind, and
come every day to my cote and woo me.

(3. 2. 414–15)

ROSALIND By my troth, and in good earnest, and so God mend me,
and by all pretty oaths that are not dangerous, *if* you break one jot
of your promise or come one minute behind your hour, I will
think you the most pathetical break-promise and the most hollow
lover and the most unworthy of her you call Rosalind that may be
chosen out of the gross band of the unfaithful: therefore beware
my censure and keep your promise.
ORLANDO With no less religion than *if* thou wert indeed my Rosalind:
so adieu.

(4. 1. 178–88)

ROSALIND ...*If* you do love Rosalind so near the heart as your gesture
cries it out, when your brother marries Aliena, shall you marry
her: I know into what straits of fortune she is driven; and it is not
impossible to me, *if* it appear not inconvenient to you, to set her
before your eyes tomorrow human as she is and without any
danger.

(5. 2. 62–8)

PHEBE *If* this be so, why blame you me to love you?
SILVIUS *If* this be so, why blame you me to love you?
ORLANDO *If* this be so, why blame you me to love you?

(5. 2. 102–6)

80

ROSALIND ...I will help you, *if* I can. I would love you, *if* I could. To-morrow meet me all together. I will marry you, *if* ever I marry woman, and I'll be married to-morrow. I will satisfy you, *if* ever I satisfied man, and you shall be married to-morrow. I will content you, *if* what pleases you contents you, and you shall be married to-morrow.

(5. 2. 111–18)

ROSALIND Patience once more, whiles our compact is urg'd.
You say, *if* I bring in your Rosalind,
You will bestow her on Orlando here?

(5. 4. 5–7)

DUKE SENIOR *If* there be truth in sight, you are my daughter.
ORLANDO *If* there be truth in sight, you are my Rosalind.
PHEBE *If* sight and shape be true,
Why then, my love adieu!

(5. 4. 117–20)

Malcolm Evans makes of Hymen's 'If truth holds true contents' (5. 4. 129) one of the central arguments in his challenging poststructuralist study of Shakespeare's plays and their critical history. It is a notoriously difficult line for editors to gloss; Evans argues that this is its point, coming where it does in this play of 'ifs' and other word-games. He points out that the ambiguities of each of the five words of the clause produces a total of seventy-two variants of meaning, 'each representing a different "If truth holds true contents"'.[10] 'Holds', for example, can signify 'supports', 'restrains', 'sustains', 'interrupts';[11] 'con-tents' is 'that which is contained' *or* 'happiness, pleasure'.[12] Hymen's line may be typically cryptic, as befits a god (or it may just be a scribal or typesetter's glitch – we have of course no manuscript to check the author's 'intentions'). But its sharing in the multivocal Ifs of the play does draw us back to a recognition of the always illusionary, always conditional ('as if') nature of theatre, and at the same time to its irreducible quality of linguistic play. Actors will come up with as many different meanings for words and lines as scholars will: this energy and multiplicity of denotation fits the image of theatre as a carnivalesque, liminal experience better than it does that of a quasi-sacred event which elevates the audience's moral lives and teaches them about 'self-knowledge', 'nature', 'atonement', and so on.

Evans continues to play his own games with the text by showing that if we take into account 'the specific languages of the theatre' – the stage/audience consciousness – we can come up with a figure of 168 permutations for the line 'If truth holds true contents': 'Hymen's "truth" burlesques the climactic moment of conventional plots by increasing the opacity of its constitutive materials and deferring further the presence of this final illumination to itself'. The upshot is a justification of the play's title: '*As You Like It* proffers a "nature" at once constructed and unmediated, "character" and its impossibility, and *carte blanche* for the distribution of ironies, or not, as you like it'.[13]

In the theatre, of course, we will hardly be aware of these complex ambiguities of the text; actors and director will already have made choices about meaning in order to tell the story that seems to them the 'true' one for that company, in that place, at that time, for that audience. But one thing we will notice, because of its dramaturgic positioning – the last words we hear in the theatre – is Rosalind's Epilogue, and that indeed does much of the work that Evans claims to find in his Derridean reading of the playtext. The Epilogue offers a final and gleefully deconstructive If:

> ROSALIND ... If I were a woman I would kiss as many of you as had beards that pleased me, complexions that liked me and breaths that I defied not.

Whether the role has been played by a woman or a boy (or a young man, as I discuss below), the effect is still the same: the speech powerfully foregrounds the constructedness of gender, which has been the plot's main engine (Rosalind the boy/girl/ boy/girl), the as-ifness of theatre, the recognition that for two hours we have been sharing both in an illusion (the story's fiction) and in the real pleasures produced by the charismatic performative abilities of actors such as the player of Rosalind. The Epilogue also does the valuable work of saying the show's over; do your bit as an audience, show us you appreciate our work and go home to your own real ('workingday') lives in the patriarchal economy – perhaps with a more sophisticated appreciation of what that 'reality' might mean. Uniquely in Shakespearean comedy, the heroine plays the final role of 'bridging' the stage-play world and the audience's real world. In this she is like Feste, or Puck, an unpredictable yet always watchable figure, inhabiting an exciting liminality. Rosalind's cross-dressing is, among other things, a variety of clowning.

MOMENT BY MOMENT[14]

Jensen's reading of the play, which stresses its nature as a series of performative events, seems to me to come closer to the phenomenology of the audience's experience in the theatre (or even an imaginative reader's experience in the study) than does the influential Barber-Frye school of literary criticism or the specific insights of the new historicists. It allows, for example, the play's rhetorical set-pieces and sparkling repartee to be received as moments of linguistic pleasure and opportunities for actors to show off, challenges to make them 'work'. 'The forest seems to provide a natural stage for such performances',[15] which are relatively inhibited and controlled in the first act's various scenes of masculine aggression and social hierarchy (Celia talks more than Rosalind in Act 1; Duke Frederick, Orlando, and the licensed jester Touchstone are the strong public performers). Rosalind gives herself licence to be the greatest talker in the forest by wittily using the stereotype of the female unbridled tongue, 'Do you not know I am a woman? When I think, I must speak' (3. 2. 245) – her verbal energy signalling the indecorous (according to Celia) sexual excitement that she feels on hearing of Orlando's manic performances as the romantic lover.

The songs, similarly, which pervade the time in the forest, work equally as a deliberate foregrounding of art, artifice, and theatricality as they do as thematic pointers. Music-making is an irrational but pleasurable human activity (there is no music in Act 1), a sign that community harmony is an ideal that can occasionally be fulfilled. But only momentarily: once again Jaques and Touchstone have parallel functions, as the first satirizes the simple-minded utopianism of 'Under the green-wood tree' (2. 5), and the second claims grumpily that 'It was a lover and his lass' is 'untuneable' and 'time lost' (5. 3. 14–43). Interestingly, the rather more cynical 'Blow, blow thou winter wind' (2. 7) is not subject to any such critique, nor is the men's hunting-song in 4. 2, with its obsessive and self-reflexive anxiety about the ambivalent significance of horns.

The final song, 'Wedding is great Juno's crown' of course sets the seal on what Hymen has already announced as the play's 'conclusion/Of these most strange events' – the multiple weddings which befit the genre of comedy. Hymen assumes an authority like that of the writer of this play: he 'knows' these characters in the way that only an author can; there is nothing else to be known, as he spells out their expected futures ('You and you no cross shall part./You and you are heart in heart', etc., 5. 4. 130 ff.) The song's harmony echoes this and ought to signal the end of the play, like the two rhyming couplets which follow it:

> DUKE SENIOR O my dear niece, welcome thou art to me,
>   Even daughter welcome, in no less degree.
> PHEBE [to Silvius] I will not eat my word; now thou art mine,
>   Thy faith my fancy to thee doth combine.

> (5. 4. 146–9)

But, astonishingly and delightfully, the end is not yet. The arrival of Jaques de Boys never fails to produce a gale of laughter in the theatre: it is a moment of such glorious unexpectedness and yet at the same time it represents the poetic justice that (if we had a chance to reflect in the plethora of performative pleasures) we would desire of this romantic comedy – the restitution of wrongs, the conversion of the wicked, the accession of wealth for the deserving. It is so gleefully audacious in exploiting the convention of *peripeteia* that the end result is once again to stress the artificiality of theatre: this is quite definitely not a simulacrum of the real world, but a product of a writer's creative imagination, the actors' embodiment of it, and the audience's willing entry into the fantasy.

Simon Phillips's production for the Sydney Theatre Company in 1996 had the comedian Paul Livingston, costumed as Will Shakespeare (who had earlier performed the role of Hymen), now feeding the lines of Jaques de Boys's speech to the actor in fresh manuscript pages dropped down to him from a perch on a huge quill-feather above the stage. Breaking the illusionistic frame and visually embodying the audience's pleasurable recognition of the arbitrariness of 'plot' and the power of the writer, this is an example of the way that contemporary critical readings of the play can be incorporated into its performance.

The performance history of any play will reflect and embody the meanings that are available to the culture that produces it. *As You Like It*, a play popular from the eighteenth century to our own day, is no exception. As a play that centres on a remarkably energetic and voluble young woman (who courts a man while pretending to be a boy), it has a particular place in a society's thinking about gender.

It was not until 1740 that the play was revived in a recognizable form, after the fashion for the urban (and urbane) comedies of the Restoration had passed. These plays had their lively witty heroines, but they despised pastoral fantasy and everything to do with 'the country'. The comedienne Hannah Pritchard was cast as the first post-Elizabethan Rosalind, and was praised for her 'natural, sprightly' performance in contrast to the 'affected' roles that Restoration plays had provided her with.[16] After this revival, the play never looked back.

'*As You Like It* was more frequently acted at Drury Lane, from 1776 to 1817, than any other Shakespeare play.'[17] The cause of this popularity was almost entirely the star quality of the Rosalind, Dora Jordan. Interestingly, these dates coincide almost exactly with the lifespan of Jane Austen, who created in Elizabeth Bennet of *Pride and Prejudice* a Rosalind-like heroine, unashamed of her physical energy and her woman's tongue. (Austen is known to have admired Jordan.) Both characters take part in a refiguring of femininity that moves away from the stereotypes of the languishing and passive female that dominated the eighteenth-century novel and the 'sentimental drama'. But when the leading Victorian actress Helen Faucit made the role her own for over forty years, she created a new figure of idealized Victorian 'womanliness' who retained the markers of upper-class behaviour which guaranteed her purity despite her ambiguously male costume (a knee-length dress with a close-fitting bodice which clearly indicated the bosom):

> In the most joyous outbursts of the sparkling fancy amid the freedom of the forest, we never miss the duke's daughter, whom, in the first act, we have seen, in the gentleness and unconscious grace of her deportment, the leading ornament of the court of her usurping uncle. She is never less than the high-born and high-bred gentle-woman.[18]

85

The most successful Rosalinds of the latter half of the century were Americans bringing a New World energy and egalitarianism back to a repressive Britain: Mary Anderson and Ada Rehan (and later it was to be one of Katharine Hepburn's most famous non-film roles). In the first half of the twentieth century the relatively greater freedoms gained by women in Britain allowed the play to flourish with sprightly but still 'feminine' Rosalinds such as Edith Evans, Athene Seyler and Peggy Ashcroft, and a setting which was as often fifteenth- to seventeenth-century France as Elizabethan England. Arden, that is to say, was closely akin to a poetical Never Land.

The play in something closer to modern dress, and thus more likely to engage the audience's attention to its problems and contradictions, had to wait till the 1960s and the beginning of the 'youth revolution' which saw Vanessa Redgrave alternating a Rosalind in denims and a worker's cap with the actress's impassioned appearances at Ban-the-Bomb marches. Redgrave's whole demeanour was youthful before it was 'feminine', physically uninhibited by the demands of decorum: 'Prone or supine, kneeling or crouching, hugging her knees, or flinging herself backwards before Orlando when in "a more coming-on disposition", she is exquisite', said one critic; 'a twentieth-century gamin, a fantasticated Bisto kid, a terror of the lower fifth.... It may be ... that "As You Like It" has had to wait until the 1960s for someone to appreciate that this is what Rosalind is.'[19] Her appearance in the last scene brought comments about her 'radiance'; this was achieved not only by her performance, but by the director's decision to employ a lighting plot which spotlit Rosalind in a sea of flickering torches in a night-time finale: it could be read as a challenge to the darkness of the patriarchal system which the young couples were about to re-enter, and to the symbolic winter which would inevitably come again. These darker aspects had been stressed earlier in the play, with a violent beginning, a wintry forest, and a striking staging of the killing of the deer which stressed the bestiality of 'men momentarily turned to wolves'.[20] It is not hard to see the resonances with a world in the grip of nuclear anxiety.

This image of threatening darkness associated with male violence and the consequent fragility of Arden's green world has been a constant in productions since the 1960s, the anxiety it produces only relieved by charismatic performances of Rosalind – embodying a faith in human intelligence and the renewing capacities of the play's mutual desire – by such actresses as Janet Suzman (RSC, 1968), Eileen Atkins (RSC, 1973) and Susan Fleetwood (RSC, 1980).[21] The emphasis in Adrian Noble's 1985 production, with Juliet Stevenson and Fiona Shaw, was on the psychological and spiritual journeys of both Rosalind and Celia, discovering the healing power of sexuality in the Jungian 'forest within', the unconscious.[22] Christine Edzard's film is less hopeful, set in the Thatcherite England of the early 1990s: Oliver and Duke Frederick are vicious businessmen (it's hard to imagine their conversion – or any reason for it), and Arden is an urban wasteland. Oliver is rescued by his brother not from wild animals but from muggers. There seems to be little attraction between Emma Croft's Rosalind and Andrew Tiernan's Orlando (who, significantly, doubles the role of Oliver, as if to suggest that his rebellion is only skin deep), since in such a setting sex is no more healing than the fast food from Audrey's snack van. Both Hymen and the Epilogue, with their various intimations of the transforming magic of theatre, are cut from the film.

Directors at mainstream theatres are still reluctant to tackle the homoerotic potential of the play – that is, to show Orlando as falling in love with the 'boy' Ganymede and what might follow from that when the boy is revealed to be a girl: a reluctant re-entry into heterosexual orthodoxy, perhaps? or joyful relief? Or, some recognition by both Rosalind and Orlando that each is bisexual – that Rosalind and Celia can continue their loving relationship, and Orlando enjoy the company of men? The text allows for all these possibilities, and more. Two famous British productions, in 1967 and 1991, have approached these issues by using an all-male cast.

Clifford Williams directing for London's National Theatre in 1967 claimed that the play's

> examination of the infinite beauty of Man in love ... takes place in an atmosphere of spiritual purity which transcends sensuality in the search for poetic sexuality. It is for this reason that I employ a male cast; so that we shall not – entranced by the surface reality – miss the interior truth.[23]

It is difficult to see how an all-male cast, with its association with the British tradition of comic 'drag', could have created 'an atmosphere of spiritual purity' out of a play which has its full share of Elizabethan sex jokes and innuendoes. Putting the actors into modern dress (a 'Carnaby Street' look) on an abstract perspex set might well have made some comment on the 1960s flirtation with androgynous sexuality, but the critics reported that Ronald Pickup's Rosalind was 'completely non-erotic',[24] and Jeremy Brett's Orlando reassuringly masculine.

Much more successful with audiences and critics was Cheek by Jowl's production, directed by Declan Donnellan in 1991, re-staged and toured around the world up to 1995. This starred Adrian Lester as Rosalind, whose tall flat-chested and bespectacled figure contrasted disconcertingly with his fussy 'feminine' gestures and kittenish movements.[25] Donnellan claimed to be exploring both historical authenticity and gender fluidity in the production, though his repeated observation that he found the theory that Shakespeare's actresses were young boys very difficult to believe sounds like special pleading on behalf of an adult homosexual stage. Inspired by the example of Japanese Kabuki actors 'transform[ing] into women', Donnellan set about using the text to explore the constructedness of masculinity and femininity.[26] Alisa Solomon writes interestingly about the production's Act 4 scene 1 in this light, with 'an apron [used] as a sign of femininity': 'the apron serves as shifting signifier, indicating domesticated femininity, marriage, gender instability, the artificiality of "woman", and, finally, the synecdoche that underlies theatrical representation in general'.[27] But, as this example indicates (and as the video confirms), it is really only 'femininity' that is being consciously played and thereby, perhaps, deconstructed (Celia's pursed lips and simpering offered a particularly irritating example of boarding-school 'drag' acting); masculinity remains natural, essential, and the ground of sexual attractiveness in what was finally a homosexual love story.[28] As Alisa Solomon writes,

> Donnellan and his fourteen athletic actors romp joyfully on the play's rampant homoeroticism.
> Rosalind...sends sparks flying when s/he leans against Celia's shoulder, or, as Ganymede, conversing with Jacques, deliciously lays a hand on his eager arm. And in scenes with Orlando, whether

dressed as girl or boy, passion is palpable – ever more so because whether Lester is dressed as girl or boy matters so little. . . . because I never thought of Lester's Rosalind (nor Celia, Phebe, and Audrey) as a woman – but always as a "woman" – the play's heterosexuality was as artificial as a Petrarchan poem, an imposed structure, its compulsoriness made to be broken, honored, as it were, only in the breeches.[29]

My suspicion is that, for all their claims to be unveiling something 'essential' and historical in *As You Like It* (Donnellan: 'it unlocks something at the heart of the play'), both these all-male productions were at base an unconscious attempt to reclaim theatrical power for men (under increasing pressure from feminism) – especially for those men educated in British public schools and at Oxford or Cambridge, traditional establishment bastions of homosociality. Peter Holland makes the same point, stressing the impossibility of separating theatrical choices from contemporary politics:

> In the continuing debate over how modern Shakespeare production might represent women, the Cheek by Jowl *As You Like It* could be seen as an extreme form of male colonialism by completely eliminating women from the practice of representation, so that they become characters, not performers, figures able to be voiced only by men. . . . the rejection of the female voice could be seen as the rejection of the particularities of female desire, its separateness absorbed within a dominant male discourse, the discourse of Shakespeare, of Donnellan and of the male cast, and by extension the discourse of a patriarchal society.[30]

Theatre that stays alive never stands still, and rarely looks back without irony: women have now an incontrovertible part to play on Shakespeare's stage; they can claim to be represented directly in texts that may have begun as male imaginings but have survived as pieces that can allow actors to do their work of embodiment, questioning and challenging dominant discourses. As long as we have gender, sexuality, power relations, literary conventions, and a need for clowns and carnival, in this text we have a play that can be performed as we like it – or as we need it.

Notes

CHAPTER 1: PROLOGUE

1. Samuel Johnson's edition of Shakespeare's works, 1765; quoted in *As You Like It*, New Variorum Edition, ed. Richard Knowles (New York: Modern Language Association, 1977), 504.
2. Gary Waller, *Shakespeare's Comedies* (London and New York: Longman, 1991), 4.
3. Ibid., 17.
4. Steven Mullaney, *The Place of the Stage* (Ann Arbor: University of Michigan Press, 1988), pp. x–xi.
5. Fiona Shaw and Juliet Stevenson, 'Celia and Rosalind in *As You Like It*', Russell Jackson and Robert Smallwood (eds), *Players of Shakespeare* 2 (Cambridge: Cambridge University Press, 1988), 63.
6. Waller, *Shakespeare's Comedies*, 10.
7. Anthony B. Dawson, 'The Impasse over the Stage', *English Literary Renaissance*, 21, 3 (Autumn 1991), 315. Dawson rightly takes his argument to its logical extreme, pointing out that the intentions of the players do not finally control the meanings read into their actions by individual members of an audience.
8. Stephen Greenblatt, *Shakespearean Negotiations* (Oxford: Clarendon Press, 1988), 12–13.
9. W. B. Worthen, *Shakespeare and the Authority of Performance* (Cambridge: Cambridge University Press, 1997), 173. This observation leads to the 'recognition...that theatrical choices arise at the intersection between the text and the formal strategies of its meaningful production as theatre' (p. 175). Thus any attempt at 'historical' performance is doomed from the outset by the meaning-making conventions shared by actors and audience, which will override such signifiers as Elizabethan costume or a reconstructed Globe stage.
10. Penny Gay, *As She Likes It: Shakespeare's Unruly Women* (London and New York: Routledge, 1994), 15.

CHAPTER 2: THERE COMES AN OLD MAN HAD THREE SONS

1. John Bowe points out that Terry Hands's 'guideline' for the 1980 RSC production was that it was 'a fairy tale'; he also comments that this opening speech can be seen as the (masculine) 'prologue' to which Rosalind refers tongue-in-cheek in her Epilogue (*Players of Shakespeare*, ed. Philip Brockbank, Cambridge University Press, Cambridge, 1985, pp. 67, 69).
2. Louis Adrian Montrose, '"The Place of a Brother" in *As You Like It*: Social Process and Comic Form', in Ivo Kamps (ed.), *Materialist Shakespeare* (London: Verso, 1995), 40.
3. Ibid., 43.
4. Oliver renounces his lands and revenues, but by the end of the play seems to be reinstated with them via the offstage conversion of Frederick.
5. Montrose, '"The Place of a Brother"', 44.
6. Ibid., 53.
7. Ibid., 63.
8. Ibid., 57.
9. Ibid., 59.
10. Ibid., 41.
11. Ibid., 65.
12. Andrew Gurr compiles and analyses the evidence about audience composition in the public playhouses in *Playgoing in Shakespeare's London* (Cambridge: Cambridge University Press, 1987), 59–79 and Appendix 1. 'There are, for instance, almost as many references to women playgoers as to the artisan and apprentice class' (p. 59).

CHAPTER 3: THE SKIRTS OF THE FOREST

1. Steven Mullaney, *The Place of the Stage: License, Play, and Power in Renaissance England* (1988; Ann Arbor: University of Michigan Press, 1995), pp. viii–x, 22.
2. Patrick Fuery and Nick Mansfield, *Cultural Studies and the New Humanities: Concepts and Controversies* (Melbourne: Oxford University Press Australia, 1997), 70.
3. Stephen Orgel, *Impersonations: The Performance of Gender in Shakespeare's England* (Cambridge: Cambridge University Press, 1996), 103 and *passim*.
4. I am indebted to Dr Tim Fitzpatrick, of the University of Sydney's Centre for Performance Studies, for his work in developing the

91

'two-door' theory, and for his specific comments on my use of it in the paragraphs which follow. Fitzpatrick's theory is explicated in 'Shakespeare's Exploitation of a Two-Door Stage: *Macbeth*': *Theatre Research International*, 20, 3 (Autumn 1995), 207–30.

5. See Agnes Latham (ed.), *As You Like It*, Arden edn (London: Methuen, 1975), Introduction, p. xxvi.

6. Richard Wilson, '"Like the old Robin Hood": *As You Like It* and the Enclosure Riots', *Shakespeare Quarterly*, 43, 1 (Spring 1992), 3–4.

7. A. Stuart Daley, 'Where are the Woods in *As You Like It*?', *Shakespeare Quarterly*, 34, 2 (Summer 1983), 175; 'The Dispraise of the Country in *As You Like It*', *Shakespeare Quarterly*, 36, 3 (Autumn 1985), 310.

8. Daley, 'Where are the Woods?', 173.

9. Ibid., 174.

10. Ibid., 173–4.

11. A medievalist colleague, Betsy S. Taylor, has pointed out to me that this convention probably comes from the Last Judgement plays, and iconographic representations in which God is seated in the centre, the saved on his right hand, the damned on his left. The saved go right, up to Heaven, the damned left, down to Hell.

12. Madeline Doran, '"Yet am I inland bred"', in James G. McManaway (ed.), *Shakespeare 400* (New York: Holt, Rinehart and Winston, 1964), 99.

13. Ibid., 104.

14. Mullaney, *Place of the Stage*, 57.

CHAPTER 4: CALL ME GANYMEDE

1. C. L. Barber, *Shakespeare's Festive Comedy* (Princeton: Princeton University Press, 1959), 15.

2. Karen Newman, *Shakespeare's Rhetoric of Comic Character: Dramatic Convention in Classical and Renaissance Comedy* (New York and London: Methuen, 1985), 96.

3. Michael Shapiro, *Gender in Play on the Shakespearean Stage* (Ann Arbor: University of Michigan Press, 1996), 126.

4. These debates are summarized in Shapiro, *Gender in Play*, Introduction; Jean Howard, *The Stage and Social Struggle in Early Modern England* (London and New York: Routledge, 1994), 159–60.

5. Stephen Orgel, *Impersonations: The Performance of Gender in Shakespeare's England* (Cambridge: Cambridge University Press, 1996), 43. See also Bruce R. Smith, *Homosexual Desire in Shakespeare's England: A Cultural Poetics* (Chicago and London: University of Chicago Press, 1991), 147–8.

6. Orgel, *Impersonations*, 28.

7. See Orgel, *Impersonations*, 64–72, for discussion of the boy players' social status.
8. Ibid., 103.
9. Ibid., 63.
10. Kathleen McLuskie, 'The Act, the Role, and the Actor: Boy Actresses on the Elizabethan Stage', *New Theatre Quarterly*, 3 (1987), 120–30; Jean Howard, *The Stage and Social Struggle*, 119–20.
11. Howard, *The Stage and Social Struggle*, 118, 120.
12. Valerie Traub, *Desire and Anxiety: Circulations of Sexuality in Shakespearean Drama* (London and New York: Routledge, 1992), 120.
13. Ibid., 122–4.
14. Ibid., 128.
15. Stephen Greenblatt, *Shakespearean Negotiations* (1998; Oxford: Clarendon Press, 1990), 89–90.
16. This experiment was carried out with professional actors at Sydney University's Centre for Performance Studies in 1996.
17. Thomas Lodge, *Rosalynd*, ed. Brian Nellist (Keele University: Ryburn Publishing, 1995), 67. Further quotations from this edition will be incorporated into the text.
18. *Rosalynd*, 75. One likes to think that the author is consciously punning on 'Lodge' here.
19. Cf. *Rosalynd*, 49: ' "And I pray you," quoth Aliena, "if your robes were off, what mettle are you made that you are so satirical against women? Is it not a foul bird defiles the own nest?" ' Shakespeare's borrowing from Lodge is obvious.

CHAPTER 5: HOW LIKE YOU THIS SHEPHERD'S LIFE?

1. David Young, *The Heart's Forest: A Study of Shakespeare's Pastoral Plays* (New Haven and London: Yale University Press, 1972), 32.
2. W. W. Greg, *Pastoral Poetry and Pastoral Drama* (1905); quoted in New Variorum *As You Like It*, ed. Richard Knowles (New York: MLA, 1977), 513.
3. 'What suffices is enough'; Lodge, *Rosalynd*, 57.
4. Audrey's other contribution to the debates embodied in pastoral and the theatre is the unwittingly ambiguous hope that 'it is no dishonest desire, to desire to be a woman of the world' (5. 3. 3–5), since the word 'world' is as slippery in its connotations as any 'poetical' metaphor: the court, the married state, prostitution, reality?

CHAPTER 6: WEDDING IS GREAT JUNO'S CROWN

1. Edward Berry, *Shakespeare's Comic Rites* (Cambridge: Cambridge University Press, 1984), 25. Berry's chapter 'Incorporations' offers a good overview of Elizabethan public wedding rituals.
2. A. Stuart Daley, 'Where Are the Woods in *As You Like It?'*, *Shakespeare Quarterly*, 34, 2 (Summer 1983), 176; he refers to a 1586 survey of country clergymen.
3. Quoted in New Variorum *As You Like It*, ed. Richard Knowles (New York: MLA, 1977) , 628–9.
4. Juliet Stevenson, commenting on Adrian Noble's 1985 RSC production, adds some further interpretive possibilities to the line: 'Celia is *appalled*, and you can play appalled on many levels, one of which is "I am certainly not going to start impersonating clergymen," or "I am not going to marry you because God knows what you might end up doing after the ceremony!" Or you can speak the line "I cannot say the words" as involving far more cost to Celia than either of those alternatives ... because I am rendered speechless by the loss of my friend' (quoted in Carol Rutter, *Clamorous Voices: Shakespeare's Women Today* (The Women's Press, London, 1988), p. 116).
5. Latham (ed.) *As You Like It*, Appendix B, Arden edn, 134–5.
6. Traub, *Desire and Anxiety: Circulations of Sexuality in Shakespearean Drama* (London and New York: Routledge, 1992), 126.
7. Virgil K. Whitaker, *Shakespeare's Use of Learning* (San Marino, CA: The Huntington Library, 1953), 184.
8. Fiona Shaw and Juliet Stevenson, 'Celia and Rosalind in *As You Like It'*, in Russell Jackson and Robert Smallwood (eds), *Players of Shakespeare 2* (Cambridge: Cambridge University Press, 1988), 70.
9. Traub, *Desire and Anxiety*, 128.

CHAPTER 7: ALL THE WORLD'S A STAGE

1. Michael Mangan, *A Preface to Shakespeare's Comedies 1594–1603* (London and New York: Longman, 1996), 82.
2. Edward Berry, *Shakespeare's Comic Rites* (Cambridge: Cambridge University Press, 1984), 112. David Wiles, *Shakespeare's Clown* (Cambridge: Cambridge University Press, 1987), also describes the clown's relation to the concept of liminality: 'Within the theatre, the clown is a liminal figure in relation to the physical margins of the stage. He locates himself in the interstices of the plot. And he dominates the liminal period of the jig, when the play gives way to ordinary living. [In *As You Like It*, this role, significantly, is taken by

Rosalind's Epilogue.] The theatre building is an almost unique gathering point where the social classes come together, and inside that building the clown separates himself from the structured language of verse, and from the structure of the narrative fiction, and appears to set up with the audience a communion of undifferentiated, equal individuals' (p. 174).

3. Ibid., 136–7.
4. For further discussion of Shakespeare's company's clowns, see Wiles, *Shakespeare's Clown*.
5. Mangan, *Preface*, 212.
6. Berry, *Shakespeare's Comic Rites*, 137.
7. For discussion of Bakhtin's theory of the 'grotesque' and 'carnivalesque' in relation to the clown see Wiles, *Shakespeare's Clown*, 175–6: 'the clown's task in performance is precisely *not* to create a character. His task is to project himself bodily, exploiting the grotesqueness of his "scurvy" face and his stunted or lumpish anatomy.'
8. Ejner J. Jensen, *Shakespeare and the Ends of Comedy* (Bloomington: Indiana University Press, 1991), 92.
9. Ibid., 92.
10. Malcolm Evans, *Signifying Nothing: Truth's True Contents in Shakespeare's Text* (Brighton: Harvester, 1986), 158; the argument begins on p. 145.
11. Ibid., 157.
12. Ibid., 150.
13. Ibid., 161–2.
14. This subheading pays homage to Ejner Jensen's revisionary work on the performative nature of the comedies and 'fundamental questions about the nature of comedy'. *As You Like It* is 'a play whose meanings have been canvassed extensively but whose comic energies as they unfold moment by moment on the stage have received far less attention' (*Shakespeare and the Ends of Comedy*, 83). However, while acknowledging the theatricality of the moments Jensen cites, my own reading – or imaginary production – of some of them differs significantly from Jensen's (e.g. the First Lord's response to Duke Senior's 'sermons in stones' speech in 2. 1). The possibilities of 'performance' are (fortunately) endless.
15. Jensen, *Shakespeare and the Ends of Comedy*, 93.
16. Michael Dobson, 'Improving on the Original: Actresses and Adaptations' in Jonathan Bate and Russell Jackson (eds), *Shakespeare: An Illustrated Stage History* (Oxford: Oxford University Press, 1996), 67–8. A more detailed survey of the stage history of the play up to 1970 can be found in the New Variorum edition (ed. Knowles), pp. 630–42; and up to 1990, in Alan Brissenden's edition of the play (World's Classics), with many illustrations, pp. 50–81.

17. Latham (ed.), *As You Like It*, Introduction to Arden edn, p. lxxxvii.
18. An 1845 review of Faucit's Rosalind, quoted in Brissenden's edition of the play, 57. G. H. Lewes commented perceptively on her costume: 'Her mannish disguise is just sufficient to warrant the illusion of her companions, yet never for an instance presents her as less than womanly. It is like a cockade upon a woman's hat, a saucy symbol of the masculine type, which makes you the more conscious of her absent masculinity' (quoted in Carol J. Carlisle, 'Helen Faucit's Rosalind', *Shakespeare Studies*, 12, 1979, pp. 79–80. Carlisle's essay emphasizes the charismatic variety of Faucit's performance.). Mary Hamer comments that 'Playing Rosalind, indeed, for [Faucit], became a positive occasion of moral improvement' ('Shakespeare's Rosalind and Her Public Image', *Theatre Research International*, vol. 11, no. 2, 1986, p. 113). Faucit disliked playing the Epilogue because of her commitment to psychological realism, but bowed to tradition. Kelly McGillis, playing Rosalind for the Shakespeare Theatre Washington's 1997 season, simply cut the Epilogue on these grounds; she claimed, 'I felt uncomfortable saying it, because you've seen a girl playing the role' (post-performance discussion with the audience, April 1997).
19. Quoted in Penny Gay, *As She Likes It: Shakespeare's Unruly Women* (London and New York: Routledge, 1994), 55. My chapter on *As You Like It* provides an analysis of the play's performance history in England since World War II.
20. Ibid., 57.
21. For a description of the much-admired 1980 production, directed by Terry Hands, see the essay by John Bowe (the Orlando), in *Players of Shakespeare*, ed. Philip Brockbank (Cambridge: Cambridge University Press, 1985), 67–76. Hands stressed the 'fairy tale' and fertility rite aspect of the play, but what came across most strongly was Rosalind and Orlando's physical attraction to each other (see my comments in *As She Likes It*, 72–5).
22. RSC 1985 programme; see also Fiona Shaw and Juliet Stevenson, 'Celia and Rosalind in *As You Like It*', *Players of Shakespeare 2* (Cambridge: Cambridge University Press, 1988), 55–71; *Clamorous Voices*, ed. Carol Rutter (London: The Women's Press, 1988), 96–121; and Adrian Noble's essay, ' "Well, This Is the Forest of Arden" ', in Werner Habicht, D. J. Palmer, Roger Pringle (eds), *Images of Shakespeare: Proceedings of the Third Congress of the International Shakespeare Association, 1986* (London and Toronto: Associated University Presses, 1988), 335–42.
23. Programme note, quoted in Gay, *As She Likes It*, 62–3.
24. Ibid., 63. A contemporary (anonymous) review of this production is reproduced in John Russell Brown (ed.), *Much Ado About Nothing and*

As You Like It: a Casebook (London: Macmillan, 1979), 239–41.

25. Lester's performance can be seen in part on a video published by Routledge; the Orlando in this 1995 remounting is a rather weedy Scott Handy, replacing the more conventionally masculine, dark and handsome Patrick Toomey who first played the role.

26. Quotations are from an interview with Declan Donnellan by Gerard Raymond, *Theater Week*, 3–9 October 1994, pp. 13–16.

27. Alisa Solomon, *Re-dressing the Canon: Essays on Theater and Gender* (London and New York: Routledge, 1997), 41.

28. Peter J. Smith, *Social Shakespeare* (Macmillan, London, 1995), who also saw this production, supports Solomon's perception of it as an openly homoerotic reading. Smith notes a consequent re-orienting of the final wedding scene: 'Orlando, with a look of utter shock, staggered back and shoved [Rosalind] from him, darting up-stage. Rejected, Rosalind had no option but to throw herself, weeping, on her father. . . . the lines became failed and then successful attempts to submit herself to male authority figures. Orlando visually recanted and walked down-stage to reclaim his wife but the damage had been done and the effect was to question the firmness of such a union' (p. 207). The production also partnered off Jaques with Amiens in its last moments.

    Peter Holland, on the other hand, felt that 'The play-acting of Rosalind/Ganymede was both more intriguing and simpler than it is when a woman plays Rosalind but the tremendous erotic charge between Rosalind and Orlando had nothing glibly homoerotic about it.' (*English Shakespeares*, Cambridge University Press, Cambridge, 1997, p. 91).

29. Solomon, *Re-Dressing the Canon*, 23, 26.

30. Holland, *English Shakespeares*, 92.

Select Bibliography

EDITIONS OF *AS YOU LIKE IT*

Gilman, Albert (ed.), *As You Like It*, The Signet Classic Shakespeare (New York: New American Library, 1963). Contains selections from Lodge's *Rosalynd*, and a selection of critical commentary from the late nineteenth century to 1959.

Latham, Agnes (ed.), *As You Like It*, The Arden Shakespeare, 3rd series (London: Methuen, 1975; repr. London and New York: Nelson, 1996). Contains a thorough introduction to the historical circumstances of the play's writing and production, including a comprehensive discussion of literary sources and analogues. (Edition used in this study.)

Knowles, Richard (ed.), *As You Like It*, New Variorum Edition (New York: Modern Language Association of America, 1977). An excellent compendium of scholarship and criticism up to the 1970s: contains an annotated text of the play, discussions of its date of composition, textual history, source materials (including a complete text of *Rosalynd*), critical history since the eighteenth century, stage history, music, and an extensive bibliography.

Brissenden, Alan (ed.), *As You Like It*, The World's Classics (Oxford and New York: Oxford University Press, 1994). The most recent scholarly edition in paperback; strong emphasis on the performance history of the play; appendix on the songs, with music.

Howard, Jean E. (ed.), *As You Like It*, in *The Norton Shakespeare*, ed. Stephen Greenblatt et al. (New York: W. W. Norton & Co., 1997). The most recent one-volume complete Shakespeare; includes introductory essays (illustrated) on Shakespeare's world, life and art, the theatrical milieu, the printed book, chronologies, and a substantial selection of relevant sixteenth- and seventeenth-century documents; up-to-date substantial bibliography.

CRITICAL STUDIES OF *AS YOU LIKE IT*

Barber, C. L., *Shakespeare's Festive Comedy: a Study of Dramatic Form and its Relation to Social Custom* (New Jersey: Princeton University Press, 1959). Still an excellent introduction to the social role and folk connections of Elizabethan comedy. Introductory chapter worth reading, also chapter on *As You Like It*, though readers should be wary of dated assumptions about the 'tone' and feeling of characters' speeches; also sees Rosalind as an embodiment of the New Critical ideal of 'poise'.

Berry, Edward, *Shakespeare's Comic Rites* (Cambridge: Cambridge University Press, 1984). Illuminatingly applies the anthropological theories of Arnold van Gennep to the pattern of the comedies, from 'rites of separation' to reincorporation in wedding, feasting, etc. 'The consistent use of symbolic geography in the plays – the movement of characters into the "holiday" or "green" worlds so important in the criticism of C. L. Barber and Northrop Frye – creates mysterious landscapes analogous to the sacred forests of initiation. In these enchanted places, Shakespeare's protagonists experience the dislocations and confusions of identity, the ordeals, and the education characteristic of the liminal phase' (p. 5).

Brockbank, Philip (ed.), *Players of Shakespeare* (Cambridge: Cambridge University Press, 1985). Contains essay by John Bowe on his Orlando (1980) – his approach to the play in an admired RSC production by Terry Hands.

Brown, John Russell (ed.) *As You Like It and Much Ado About Nothing: A Casebook* (London: Macmillan, 1979). Contains a representation of the best criticism before 1980: essays by Helen Gardner, Sylvan Barnet, David Young, D. J. Palmer. Also includes some reviews of modern performances.

Bulman, James C. (ed.) *Shakespeare, Theory and Performance* (London and New York: Routledge, 1996). Nothing specific on *As You Like It*, but a stimulating collection of essays from contemporary critical perspectives; Bulman's 'Shakespeare and performance theory', Worthen's 'Staging "Shakespeare"': acting, authority, and the rhetoric of performance' are particularly recommended.

Carlson, Susan, *Women and Comedy: Rewriting the British Theatrical Tradition* (Ann Arbor: University of Michigan Press, 1991). Chapter on 'Shakespeare's Rosalind: The Strong Woman in the Comic Tradition'. A reading which stresses the containment of Rosalind by the patriarchy; interesting on her linguistic power and her closeness to Celia.

Crowl, Samuel, *Shakespeare Observed: Studies in Performance on Stage and*

Screen (Athens, Ohio: Ohio University Press, 1992). Adrian Noble's 1985 RSC production described, pp. 132–41.

Dawson, Anthony B., *Watching Shakespeare: A Playgoers' Guide* (London: Macmillan, 1988). Chapter on *As You Like It* describes in imaginative detail some of the theatrical potential of the play, with reference to various productions.

Doran, Madeline, ' "Yet am I inland bred" ', in James G. McManaway, (ed.), *Shakespeare 400* (New York: Holt, Rinehart and Winston, 1964). A subtle analysis of the pastoral theme of Nature vs. Art.

Erickson, Peter, *Patriarchal Structures in Shakespeare's Drama* (Berkeley and Los Angeles: University of California Press, 1985). Chapter on 'Sexual Politics and Social Structure in *As You Like It*' gives an analysis (via close reading) of gender/power interplay in the play's structure. 'In the boy-actor motif, woman is a metaphor for the male discovery of the feminine within himself, of those qualities suppressed by a masculinity strictly defined as aggressiveness. Once the tenor of the metaphor has been attained, the vehicle can be discarded – just as Rosalind is discarded. The sense of the patriarchal ending in *AYL* is that male androgyny is affirmed whereas female "liberty" in the person of Rosalind is curtailed' (pp. 34–5).

Evans, Malcolm, *Signifying Nothing: Truth's True Contents in Shakespeare's Text* (Brighton: Harvester, 1986). Stimulating application of post-structuralist theory to *As You Like It* (pp. 145–62). Witty and readable; focuses on speeches of Duke Senior, Jaques, and Hymen. Provocative revision of 'simplistic' liberal humanist view of Shakespeare.

Gay, Penny, *As She Likes It: Shakespeare's Unruly Women* (London and New York: Routledge, 1994). Chapter on 'Who's Who in the Greenwood' analyses the performance history of *As You Like It* at the Royal Shakespeare Theatre, 1952–1990, with particular attention to the representation of gender in Rosalind and Orlando.

Holland, Peter, *English Shakespeares* (Cambridge: Cambridge University Press, 1997). Includes detailed and thought-provoking reviews of recent productions of *As You Like It*.

Jackson, Russell and Smallwood, Robert (eds), *Players of Shakespeare 2* (Cambridge: Cambridge University Press, 1988). Essays by Alan Rickman on Jaques, and Fiona Shaw and Juliet Stevenson on Celia and Rosalind in Adrian Noble's 1985 RSC production: explores the theme of the girls' friendship with great subtlety and sensitivity.

Jackson, Russell and Smallwood, Robert (eds), *Players of Shakespeare 3* (Cambridge: Cambridge University Press, 1993). Contains essay by Sophie Thompson on playing Rosalind for the RSC in 1989 and Celia in an earlier production; thoughtful, especially on Rosalind's 'journey' and on the darkness of both court and forest: 'I was in a dress at the beginning, then I found a new kind of freedom ... and now as we move towards the ending I have to go back to the court and the court clothes, as though something is closed off again' (p. 83).

Jensen, Ejner J., *Shakespeare and the Ends of Comedy* (Bloomington: Indiana University Press, 1991). Radical critique of the critical tradition, especially the dominance of the 'Barber-Frye' school of thought which privileges teleological readings of plays – i.e. the end is the most important moment of the play, in which its meaning will finally be seen. Gives his own view of the 'arresting theatrical pleasure everywhere available in the comedies' (p. 19).

Kennedy, Dennis, *Looking at Shakespeare: A Visual History of Twentieth-century Performance* (Cambridge: Cambridge University Press, 1993). Pages 257–65 give a brief overview of changes in production styles of *As You Like It* up to 1977; particularly interesting on Peter Stein's epic deconstructive West Berlin production (1977): 'By using an environmental setting that required the spectator's participation, Stein made the spectator part of the court, part of the forest, and part of the journey between them' (p. 265).

Leggatt, Alexander, *Shakespeare's Comedy of Love* (London and New York: Methuen, 1974). Chapter on *As You Like It* still a helpful reading of the play, aware of its stage dimension.

Mangan, Michael, *A Preface to Shakespeare's Comedies 1594–1603* (London and New York: Longman, 1996). Clear and helpful coverage of contemporary critical and historical discussions of the comedies, with an emphasis on original stage-audience relation; includes a separate chapter on *As You Like It*.

Montrose, Louis Adrian, '"The Place of a Brother" in *As You Like It*: Social Process and Comic Form', in Ivo Kamps (ed.) *Materialist Shakespeare* (London: Verso, 1995). A convenient reprinting of Montrose's seminal new historicist study of the play (1981).

Nevo, Ruth, *Comic Transformations in Shakespeare* (London: Methuen, 1980). In *As You Like It* Rosalind and Orlando discover different versions of their Act 1 selves via 'inspired improvisation, the capacity to seize and make the most of one's comic opportuni-ties.... What [the play] embodies in its trickster heroine is comic pleasure itself, in practice and in action: a liberating playful fantasy, an expansive reconciliation of opportunities of all kinds, enlivening and enchanting' (p. 181).

Newman, Karen, *Shakespeare's Rhetoric of Comic Character: Dramatic Convention in Classical and Renaissance Comedy* (New York and London: Methuen, 1985). Stresses the performative/rhetorical rather than the psychological theory of dramatic 'character': 'we learn about Rosalind and the other characters ... through their interaction . . . and the contrasting of one attitude with another' (p. 94).

Noble, Adrian, ' "Well, This Is the Forest of Arden" ', in Werner Habicht, et al. (eds), *Images of Shakespeare: Proceedings of the Third Congress of the International Shakespeare Association, 1986* (London and Toronto: Associated University Presses, 1988). Noble ruminates informally on issues arising from his production of *As You Like It*.

Rutter, Carol, *Clamorous Voices: Shakespeare's Women Today* (London: The Women's Press, 1988). Chapter on 'Rosalind: Iconoclast in Arden' comprising a discussion with Fiona Shaw, Juliet Stevenson, and Sinead Cusack. An illuminating analysis of modern actresses' approaches to Celia and Rosalind – their friendship, and the gender issues in the play.

Salingar, Leo, *Shakespeare and the Traditions of Comedy* (Cambridge: Cambridge University Press, 1974). Helpful formalist analysis of the modes of comedy up to and including Shakespeare; *As You Like It* as a 'discussion' of Ovidian themes, pp. 287–99.

Shapiro, Michael, *Gender in Play on the Shakespearean Stage* (Ann Arbor: University of Michigan Press, 1996). Useful introduction discussing the current approaches to boy-actresses in clear terms; chapter on *As You Like It*, 'Layers of Disguise', returns the issue to its arguable effect in the theatre with commentary on key scenes.

Smith, Peter J., *Social Shakespeare* (Basingstoke: Macmillan, 1995). Chapter on 'Playing with Boys' is a clear and sensible survey of the historical material re sixteenth-century homosexuality and modern attempts to deal with this aspect of Shakespeare. Thought-provoking introduction and ch. 1, 'Shakespeare's Comedy of Consensus': 'Fashion implies a knowing assent to social and cultural structures and the heroes and heroines of Shakespearean comedies are, for this reason, natty dressers' (p. 30).

Solomon, Alisa, *Re-dressing the Canon: Essays on Theater and Gender* (London and New York: Routledge, 1997). Chapter on 'Much virtue in If: Shakespeare's cross-dressed boy-actresses' takes off from the writer's experience of watching the Cheek by Jowl all-male production into a lively exploration of the boy-actress on the Elizabethan stage and thence into the nature of the illusionary theatre, then and now. Thought-provoking in raising questions about the play in the theatre.

Traub, Valerie, *Desire and Anxiety: Circulations of Sexuality in Shakespearean Drama* (London and New York: Routledge, 1992). Chapter on 'The homoerotics of Shakespearean comedy' is a somewhat challenging read (some modern critical jargon may need explanation), but ultimately very helpful in pointing to ways of reading the play's eroticism; summarizes the arguments over the effect of boy-actresses.

Waller, Gary (ed.), *Shakespeare's Comedies* (London: Longman, 1991). Introduction gives a clear and comprehensive overview of recent critical approaches; particularly helpful on new historicism and cultural materialism. Collection reprints Peter B. Erickson's chapter on *As You Like It* from *Patriarchal Structures in Shakespearean Drama*.

Ward, John Powell, *Twayne's New Critical Introductions to Shakespeare, As You Like It* (New York: Twayne Publishers, 1992). Lively introductory essay on the critical tradition, with some reference to performance history. Witty and off-beat reading of various thematic nodes: non-action; trees talking; poetry/lies/truth; 'If'. Rather too speculative, little attention to dramatic and theatrical potential.

Wofford, Susanne L., ' "To you I give myself, for I am yours": Erotic performance and theatrical performatives in *As You Like It*', in Russ McDonald (ed.), *Shakespeare Reread: The Texts in New Contexts* (Ithaca and London: Cornell University Press, 1994), 147–69. A difficult piece, but touches on important matters, particularly the performative power of theatre for the audience (i.e. how much it 'makes real' an alternative system).

Young, David, *The Heart's Forest: A Study of Shakespeare's Pastoral Plays* (New Haven and London: Yale University Press, 1972). Excellent introduction on pastoral literature; chapter on *As You Like It* a subtle reading of the play's use of pastoral: 'uniqueness grounded in its attitude toward the convention on which it is based ... treatment of nature, its self-consciousness, its emphasis on relativity, subjectivity, and paradox, its continual shifting of attitudes and judgements, and its generalizing tendencies' (pp. 70–71).

BACKGROUND READING

Shakespeare's Life, Background and Reputation

Bate, Jonathan, *The Genius of Shakespeare* (London: Picador, 1997). A lively introduction to the known facts of Shakespeare's life, his plays, and his enduring reputation as a 'genius'. Rosalind's 'true originality is that she improvises her own identity. And that is why actors, audiences, readers have kept on coming back to her for four hundred years' (p. 144).

Schoenbaum, Samuel, *William Shakespeare: A Documentary Life* (Oxford: Oxford University Press, 1975; rev. edn 1987). Surveys all available documentary evidence.

Wells, Stanley, *Shakespeare: The Poet and his Plays* (London: Methuen, 1997). Introductory chapters 'Who is Shakespeare?' and 'Shakespeare: Man of the Theatre' sketch his life; following chapters discuss the plays in groups chronologically.

Wells, Stanley (ed.), *The Cambridge Companion to Shakespeare Studies* (Cambridge: Cambridge University Press, 1986). Essays covering all the basic information about Shakespeare's life and work.

Shakespeare's Theatre

Gurr, Andrew, *Playgoing in Shakespeare's London* (Cambridge: Cambridge University Press, 1987). Survey of all available evidence about the first audiences of the plays (including those by authors other than Shakespeare).

Gurr, Andrew, *The Shakespearean Stage 1574–1642* (Cambridge: Cambridge University Press, 3rd edn, 1992). Survey of all available evidence about the London theatre of Shakespeare's day; updated with reference to recent archeological discoveries.

Schoenbaum, Samuel, *Shakespeare, The Globe, and the World* (New York and London: The Folger Shakespeare Library, 1979). Contains a good selection of historic illustrations.

Thomson, Peter, *Shakespeare's Professional Career* (Cambridge: Cambridge University Press, 1992). Detailed analysis of the theatrical milieu in which Shakespeare worked.

Thomson, Peter, *Shakespeare's Theatre* (London and New York: Routledge, 2nd edn, 1992). Concentrates on the Globe and its plays, using *Twelfth Night*, *Hamlet*, and *Macbeth* as practical examples.

Wiles, David, *Shakespeare's Clown* (Cambridge: Cambridge University Press, 1987). A mine of information on the professional clowns of Shakespeare's theatre; interesting speculations on Touchstone's name and on 'motley wear'.

Shakespeare and New Historicism

Greenblatt, Stephen, *Shakespearean Negotiations* (Oxford: Clarendon Press, 1988). Chapters on 'The Circulation of Social Energy' and 'Fiction and Friction' offer illuminating new ways of thinking about the comedies in the context of Elizabethan society. Comments on Rosalind's 'improvisational self-fashioning', pp. 90–91.

Howard, Jean E., *The Stage and Social Struggle in Early Modern England* (London and New York: Routledge, 1994). Chapters on 'The Materiality of Ideology' and 'Power and Eros' are particularly interesting on women at the theatre and the question of cross-dressing.

Jardine, Lisa, *Still Harping on Daughters: Women and Drama in the Age of Shakespeare* (New York and London: Harvester Wheatsheaf, 1983; 2nd edn 1989). Although it has little specifically on *As You Like It* (mostly in ch. 1 on 'female roles and Elizabethan eroticism'), this remains a thorough introduction to the situation of women in Elizabethan society; argues that drama reflects and complicates the official discourse of patriarchy.

Mullaney, Steven, *The Place of the Stage: License, Play, and Power in Renaissance England* (Chicago: University of Chicago Press, 1988; repr. Ann Arbor: University of Michigan Press, 1995). A study of the intersections of theatre and civic authority.

Orgel, Stephen, *Impersonations: The Performance of Gender in Shakespeare's England* (Cambridge: Cambridge University Press, 1996). Examines the representation of gender through the question, 'Why was England the only country in Europe to maintain an all-male public theatre in the Renaissance?'

Index

Recent and Forthcoming Titles in the New Series of

WRITERS AND THEIR WORK

"...this series promises to outshine its own previously high reputation."
Times Higher Education Supplement

"...will build into a fine multi-volume critical encyclopaedia of English literature."
Library Review & Reference Review

"...Excellent, informative, readable, and recommended."
NATE News

"written by outstanding contemporary critics, whose expertise is flavoured by unashamed enthusiasm for their subjects and the series' diverse aspirations."
Times Educational Supplement

"A useful and timely addition to the ranks of the lit crit and reviews genre. Written in an accessible and authoritative style."
Library Association Record

WRITERS AND THEIR WORK

RECENT & FORTHCOMING TITLES

Title	Author
Chinua Achebe	*Nahem Yousaf*
Peter Ackroyd	*Susana Onega*
Fleur Adcock	*Janet Wilson*
Kingsley Amis	*Richard Bradford*
Anglo-Saxon Verse	*Graham Holderness*
Antony and Cleopatra 2/e	*Ken Parker*
Matthew Arnold	*Kate Campbell*
As You Like It	*Penny Gay*
Margaret Atwood	*Marion Wynne-Davies*
W. H. Auden	*Stan Smith*
Jane Austen	*Robert Miles*
Alan Ayckbourn	*Michael Holt*
J. G. Ballard	*Michel Delville*
Pat Barker	*Sharon Monteith*
Djuna Barnes	*Deborah Parsons*
Julian Barnes	*Matthew Pateman*
Samuel Beckett	*Sinead Mooney*
Aphra Behn 2/e	*S. J. Wiseman*
John Betjeman	*Dennis Brown*
William Blake	*Steven Vine*
Edward Bond	*Michael Mangan*
Anne Brontë	*Betty Jay*
Emily Brontë	*Stevie Davies*
Robert Browning	*John Woolford*
A. S. Byatt	*Richard Todd*
Byron	*Drummond Bone*
Caroline Drama	*Julie Sanders*
Angela Carter 2/e	*Lorna Sage*
Bruce Chatwin	*Kerry Featherstone*
Geoffrey Chaucer	*Steve Ellis*
Children's Literature	*Kimberley Reynolds*
Caryl Churchill 2/e	*Elaine Aston*
John Clare	*John Lucas*
Arthur Hugh Clough	*John Schad*
S. T. Coleridge	*Stephen Bygrave*
Joseph Conrad	*Cedric Watts*
Coriolanus	*Anita Pacheco*
Stephen Crane	*Kevin Hayes*
Crime Fiction	*Martin Priestman*
Anita Desai	*Elaine Ho*
Shashi Deshpande	*Armrita Bhalla*
Charles Dickens	*Rod Mengham*
John Donne	*Stevie Davies*
Margaret Drabble	*Glenda Leeming*
John Dryden	*David Hopkins*
Carol Ann Duffy 2/e	*Deryn Rees Jones*
Douglas Dunn	*David Kennedy*
Early Modern Sonneteers	*Michael Spiller*
George Eliot	*Josephine McDonagh*
T. S. Eliot	*Colin MacCabe*
English Translators of Homer	*Simeon Underwood*
J. G. Farrell	*John McLeod*

RECENT & FORTHCOMING TITLES

Title	Author
Henry Fielding	*Jenny Uglow*
Veronica Forrest-Thomson – Language Poetry	*Alison Mark*
E. M. Forster	*Nicholas Royle*
John Fowles	*William Stephenson*
Brian Friel	*Geraldine Higgins*
Athol Fugard	*Dennis Walder*
Elizabeth Gaskell	*Kate Flint*
The *Gawain*-Poet	*John Burrow*
The Georgian Poets	*Rennie Parker*
William Golding 2/e	*Kevin McCarron*
Graham Greene	*Peter Mudford*
Neil M. Gunn	*J. B. Pick*
Ivor Gurney	*John Lucas*
Hamlet 2/e	*Ann Thompson & Neil Taylor*
Thomas Hardy 2/e	*Peter Widdowson*
Tony Harrison	*Joe Kelleher*
William Hazlitt	*J. B. Priestley; R. L. Brett (intro. by Michael Foot)*
Seamus Heaney 2/e	*Andrew Murphy*
George Herbert	*T.S. Eliot (intro. by Peter Porter)*
Geoffrey Hill	*Andrew Roberts*
Gerard Manley Hopkins	*Daniel Brown*
Ted Hughes	*Susan Bassnett*
Henrik Ibsen 2/e	*Sally Ledger*
Kazuo Ishiguro 2/e	*Cynthia Wong*
Henry James – The Later Writing	*Barbara Hardy*
James Joyce 2/e	*Steven Connor*
Julius Caesar	*Mary Hamer*
Franz Kafka	*Michael Wood*
John Keats	*Kelvin Everest*
James Kelman	*Gustav Klaus*
Rudyard Kipling	*Jan Montefiore*
Hanif Kureishi	*Ruvani Ranasinha*
Samuel Johnson	*Liz Bellamy*
William Langland: *Piers Plowman*	*Claire Marshall*
King Lear	*Terence Hawkes*
Philip Larkin 2/e	*Laurence Lerner*
D. H. Lawrence	*Linda Ruth Williams*
Doris Lessing	*Elizabeth Maslen*
C. S. Lewis	*William Gray*
Wyndham Lewis and Modernism	*Andrzej Gasiorek*
David Lodge	*Bernard Bergonzi*
Katherine Mansfield	*Andrew Bennett*
Christopher Marlowe	*Thomas Healy*
Andrew Marvell	*Annabel Patterson*
Ian McEwan 2/e	*Kiernan Ryan*
Measure for Measure	*Kate Chedgzoy*
The Merchant of Venice	*Warren Chernaik*
Middleton and His Collaborators	*Hutchings & Bromham*
A Midsummer Night's Dream	*Helen Hackett*
John Milton	*Nigel Smith*
Alice Munro	*Ailsa Cox*
Vladimir Nabokov	*Neil Cornwell*

RECENT & FORTHCOMING TITLES

Title	Author
V. S. Naipaul	*Suman Gupta*
New Woman Writers	*Marion Shaw/Lyssa Randolph*
Grace Nichols	*Sarah Lawson-Welsh*
Edna O'Brien	*Amanda Greenwood*
Flann O'Brien	*Joe Brooker*
Ben Okri	*Robert Fraser*
George Orwell	*Douglas Kerr*
Othello	*Emma Smith*
Walter Pater	*Laurel Brake*
Brian Patten	*Linda Cookson*
Caryl Phillips	*Helen Thomas*
Harold Pinter	*Mark Batty*
Sylvia Plath 2/e	*Elisabeth Bronfen*
Pope Amongst the Satirists	*Brean Hammond*
Revenge Tragedies of the Renaissance	*Janet Clare*
Jean Rhys 2/e	*Helen Carr*
Richard II	*Margaret Healy*
Richard III	*Edward Burns*
Dorothy Richardson	*Carol Watts*
John Wilmot, Earl of Rochester	*Germaine Greer*
Romeo and Juliet	*Sasha Roberts*
Christina Rossetti	*Kathryn Burlinson*
Salman Rushdie 2/e	*Damian Grant*
Paul Scott	*Jacqueline Banerjee*
The Sensation Novel	*Lyn Pykett*
P. B. Shelley	*Paul Hamilton*
Sir Walter Scott	*Harriet Harvey Wood*
Iain Sinclair	*Robert Sheppard*
Christopher Smart	*Neil Curry*
Wole Soyinka	*Mpalive Msiska*
Muriel Spark	*Brian Cheyette*
Edmund Spenser	*Colin Burrow*
Gertrude Stein	*Nicola Shaughnessy*
Laurence Sterne	*Manfred Pfister*
Bram Stoker	*Andrew Maunder*
Graham Swift	*Peter Widdowson*
Jonathan Swift	*Ian Higgins*
Swinburne	*Catherine Maxwell*
Elizabeth Taylor	*N. R. Reeve*
Alfred Tennyson	*Seamus Perry*
W. M. Thackeray	*Richard Salmon*
D. M. Thomas	*Bran Nicol*
Three Lyric Poets	*William Rowe*
J. R. R. Tolkien	*Charles Moseley*
Leo Tolstoy	*John Bayley*
Charles Tomlinson	*Tim Clark*
Anthony Trollope	*Andrew Sanders*
Victorian Quest Romance	*Robert Fraser*
Marina Warner	*Laurence Coupe*
Edith Wharton	*Janet Beer*
Oscar Wilde	*Alexandra Warrick*
Angus Wilson	*Peter Conradi*
Mary Wollstonecraft	*Jane Moore*
Women's Gothic 2/e	*E. J. Clery*

RECENT & FORTHCOMING TITLES

Title	Author
Women Poets of the 19th Century	*Emma Mason*
Women Romantic Poets	*Anne Janowitz*
Women Writers of Children's Classics	*Mary Sebag-Montefiore*
Women Writers of the 17th Century	*Ramona Wray*
Virginia Woolf 2/e	*Laura Marcus*
Working Class Fiction	*Ian Haywood*
W. B. Yeats	*Edward Larrissy*
Charlotte Yonge	*Alethea Hayter*
Ama Ata Aidoo	*Nana Wilson-Tagoe*
John Banville	*Peter Dempsey*
William Barnes	*Christopher Ricks*
Black British Writers	*Deidre Osborne*
Charlotte Brontë	*Stevie Davies*
Basil Bunting	*Martin Stannard*
John Bunyan	*Tamsin Spargoe*
Cymbeline	*Peter Swaab*
David Edgar	*Peter Boxall*
Nadine Gordimer	*Lewis Nkosi*
Geoffrey Grigson	*R. M. Healey*
David Hare	*Jeremy Ridgman*
The Imagist Poets	*Andrew Thacker*
Ben Jonson	*Anthony Johnson*
A. L. Kennedy	*Dorothy McMillan*
Jack Kerouac	*Michael Hrebebiak*
Jamaica Kincaid	*Susheila Nasta*
Rosamond Lehmann	*Judy Simon*
Una Marson & Louise Bennett	*Alison Donnell*
Norman MacCaig	*Alasdair Macrae*
Much Ado About Nothing	*John Wilders*
R. K. Narayan	*Shirley Chew*
Ngugi wa Thiong'o	*Brendon Nicholls*
Religious Poets of the 17th Century	*Helen Wilcox*
Samuel Richardson	*David Deeming*
Olive Schreiner	*Carolyn Burdett*
Sam Selvon	*Ramchand & Salick*
Olive Senior	*Denise de Caires Narain*
Mary Shelley	*Catherine Sharrock*
Charlotte Smith & Helen Williams	*Angela Keane*
R. L. Stevenson	*David Robb*
Tom Stoppard	*Nicholas Cadden*
Dylan Thomas	*Chris Wiggington*
Three Avant-Garde Poets	*Peter Middleton*
Derek Walcott	*Stephen Regan*
Jeanette Winterson	*Gina Vitello*
Women's Poetry at the Fin de Siècle	*Anna Vadillo*
William Wordsworth	*Nicola Trott*

TITLES IN PREPARATION

Title	Author
Ama Ata Aidoo	*Nana Wilson-Tagoe*
John Banville	*Peter Dempsey*
William Barnes	*Christopher Ricks*
Black British Writers	*Deidre Osborne*
Charlotte Brontë	*Stevie Davies*
Basil Bunting	*Martin Stannard*
John Bunyan	*Tamsin Spargoe*
Cymbeline	*Peter Swaab*
David Edgar	*Peter Boxall*
Nadine Gordimer	*Lewis Nkosi*
Geoffrey Grigson	*R. M. Healey*
David Hare	*Jeremy Ridgman*
The Imagist Poets	*Andrew Thacker*
Ben Jonson	*Anthony Johnson*
A. L. Kennedy	*Dorothy McMillan*
Jack Kerouac	*Michael Hrebebiak*
Jamaica Kincaid	*Susheila Nasta*
Rosamond Lehmann	*Judy Simon*
Una Marson & Louise Bennett	*Alison Donnell*
Norman MacCaig	*Alasdair Macrae*
Much Ado About Nothing	*John Wilders*
R. K. Narayan	*Shirley Chew*
Ngugi wa Thiong'o	*Brendon Nicholls*
Religious Poets of the 17th Century	*Helen Wilcox*
Samuel Richardson	*David Deeming*
Olive Schreiner	*Carolyn Burdett*
Sam Selvon	*Ramchand & Salick*
Olive Senior	*Denise de Caires Narain*
Mary Shelley	*Catherine Sharrock*
Charlotte Smith & Helen Williams	*Angela Keane*
R. L. Stevenson	*David Robb*
Tom Stoppard	*Nicholas Cadden*
Dylan Thomas	*Chris Wiggington*
Three Avant-Garde Poets	*Peter Middleton*
Derek Walcott	*Stephen Regan*
Jeanette Winterson	*Gina Vitello*
Women's Poetry at the Fin de Siècle	*Anna Vadillo*
William Wordsworth	*Nicola Trott*

Printed in the United Kingdom
by Lightning Source UK Ltd.
123842UK00001B/364-474/A